AF868713

SUCCESS MULTIPLIED

How to Multiply Your Business 10X, Live the Fastest Way Humanly Possible & Live a Regret-Free Life

Randy Wagner

© Copyright 2021 Randy Wagner -All rights reserved.

No part of this publication may be reproduced, duplicated, or transmitted in any form, including electronic or printed. Recording this publication is strictly prohibited, and any storage of this document is not allowed unless with written permission from the publisher.

ISBN (Ebook): 978-1-955553-11-7
ISBN (Paperback): 978-1-955553-10-0
ISBN (Hardback): 978-1-955553-09-4
Library of Congress Cataloging: 2021923779

Disclaimer Notice:

Please note the information contained within this document is for educational and entertainment purposes only. All effort has been executed to present accurate, up-to-date, reliable, and complete information. No warranties of any kind are declared or implied. Readers acknowledge that the author does not render legal, financial, medical, or professional advice.

Table Of Contents

"Without continual growth and progress, such words as improvement, achievement, and success have no meaning."-Benjamin Franklin

---

Introduction

A study conducted in 2019 by Gallup World Poll shows that many people show fewer signs of happiness and well-being worldwide as their lives get more miserable. The result of the study, which was put together in the World Happiness Report, reveals that overall life happiness took a 6% plunge, particularly in the United States, between 2007 and 2018. The report further shows that such unhealthiness results from many people being trapped in their stressful life routines, which hinders them from establishing the right priorities and taking the right actions for a successful life.

Let's face it—we live in a highly competitive space where everyone wants to be a winner. I have never met anyone who wants to fail. And I'm sure you haven't, either. Sadly, I have seen that most people think achieving their business and life goals involves big decisions. However, it's the small steps they take every day that matter.

When I started my first business, I was a teenager passionate about financial literacy and money management. I wasn't eager to get rich or reinvent the financial industry. I was just a boy who enjoyed his hobbies and sought an excellent way to do them. I didn't think of it as a business. It was just a way to keep my passion alive. They say it doesn't work when you work on what you like. But I enjoyed it, so I continually expanded my knowledge and made money. It was never a job for me. The more I grew with my hobby, the more inspired I became. Thus, my childhood experience was a decisive moment in my life.

I can't honestly say that all my ventures succeeded without hard work. In fact, they all required a considerable investment in time and energy. But I can say that all I had to do was step up to become the CEO (Chief Executive Officer) of the privately owned company called me with the sole mission of winning more and losing less in everything I did. And it's this journey of mine. I want to share this journey with you in this book to help you take charge of your business and personal life the fastest way possible. Like me, I want you to develop new acts of creation, explore ideas, and test your abilities.

Success Multiplied invites you to take charge of your career and become the CEO of your business and life. It inspires you to step in and attain a degree of commitment in action. This book focuses on you, as every page is designed to guide you in exploring yourself in a different dimension to make the small changes that can make a big difference in the improvement and achievement of good results.

I have divided the book into three parts to simplify your learning process. While part 1 (chapters 1-7) features what you must do to increase your business prospects and improve your chances of success, part 2 (chapters 8-14) highlights the steps you must take to maintain your success. Finally, part 3 (chapters 15-17) features the basics of creating multiple passive income streams.

If you're already on the path to achieving greatness, some of the stories and experiences inside this book will encourage and inform you. Altogether, you will learn how to move from that level of struggling to achieve exponential success in your business and life. I know you've got big-money goals; you want to achieve them and become a powerful and successful entrepreneur doing incredible things! And this book will give you all the best possible options and opportunities!

For several years, I have led strategy sessions for top business executives in renowned organizations with a mission to improve individual performance and business results. These business programs and my upbringing and field experiences have provided the insights to develop *Success Multiplied*!

And here is my promise, which is your payoff: every idea, tip, and suggestion in this book is focused on helping you improve your performance and results. Everything you find here results from many years of research, interviews, and personal experience. I know it works because I've watched it work for others, and it has worked for me too. So, the content here is not theory; I guarantee you will learn something.

So, what are you waiting for?

Let's get started!

Part I: The Inner Work

Believe in yourself. Believe in yourself because your voice is essential because your dreams matter. After all, there is only one you because you are worth it.-Anonymous

CHAPTER ONE

The Lion in You-C'mon Roarrr

Have you ever wondered why some people seem to get whatever they want while you don't? Why do some people seem to get all the breaks, while life for you looks just one issue after another? Why do some people get to build significant connections with people and excel in their business, while you can't even boast of having two friends?

Then you start to think, "No wonder they're happy; would I be happy if I did like they are doing?" "Sure," you reply, "Hasn't everyone thought that way at times?" And I guess you'd be right; everyone probably has. We've all found ourselves, at times, doubting our abilities and what we can achieve in both our business and personal lives. However, the real question is, what do we do about it when we begin to think this way?

People said I was a very old soul when I was a little boy. That meant they thought I was calm and mature beyond my age. If I seemed clear, I was trying to figure things out, and I knew I needed to be peaceful in my mind to do that. I was calm, too, because I was always aware that I was a part of an incredible universe, and I thought that meant I was necessary—just because I was here. I wanted to believe in myself as a part of this vast world, but I had to sift through a lot of nonsense before I could do that.

There was a lot of craziness in the pulsing center of New York City, where I grew up. Like large cities everywhere, New York had its share of shady characters. In my neighborhood, you're exposed to different things and start to feel like they're all good, whereas they aren't. It took a lot of mental work and practice not to let any of it break my spirit because I knew it wouldn't add any real meaning to my life.

Everywhere I turned, the world's dark nonsense got increasingly sophisticated—prejudices between races, religions, genders, and economic classes; corrupt politics and businesses. There were other things to watch out for, like too much partying, drug abuse, and gangs; crazy TV shows, movies, and music that encouraged me to be cocky, slutty, or darkly powerful; getting involved in gossip or harsh criticism. How would any of these things help me learn to truly love myself and others in a way that would make my life more joyful, productive, and rewarding?

Learning true self-love and the proper use of power was a lengthy process for me because of all of these mixed messages about how to live. It's hard to believe in yourself or know what to place value in, especially in a place where there is so much to deal with.

I didn't know what to do with myself for a long time. I knew something was missing, but I didn't know what. I knew I didn't feel whole, but I didn't know why or where to start to achieve a feeling of wholeness. I didn't think I suffered from low self-esteem because of societal imbalances. Unfortunately, this affected my life and business too. But through a process of elimination, I knew I had to feel right with myself. Before anything else could work, I had to like who I was and what I stood for. I knew that the stuff that was going on around me wasn't who I wanted to be.

So I began to dig deep. I discovered that life was entirely filled with light or darkness, and I wanted to choose actions that radiated light.

I began to watch closely and listen carefully to everyone and everything around me. I investigated it further when I came across something that had a spark of truth or light or looked more like what I wanted my life to be.

I learned how to ask the right questions about myself and other people. As I met positive friends, teachers, and counselors along the way, I made their positive qualities a part of me. I drilled them, and when I had a quiet moment, I analyzed their responses carefully. I read the books they recommended and studied those too.

I gradually started learning how to cope with this world and my situation by focusing on the positive aspects of life and discovering and developing my talents (I was learning to love myself!). Gradually, coping became easier as I realized I could improve my life. I put my attention and energy into change instead of sorrow. There is no other way to overcome disappointing relationships or the atrocities of this world. As I saw the results of my efforts, my confidence grew.

Do You Believe in Yourself?

Back then, when I was trying to figure out how to deal with all of life's adversities, somewhere deep down inside me, I knew there had to be more to life. I knew I didn't have the whole story yet. Occasionally, I'd get frustrated and impatient with my life station, then rationalize it by saying it's okay to play certain games to gain more comfort and status. After all, I saw people around me and movie characters doing this. I only had to do that a few times to know it was a huge mistake. The better part of my conscience made me feel uncomfortable and ashamed whenever I did something cruel. I knew that hurting others was not the way to find genuine happiness in my life, and it certainly wasn't the way for me to get the best results.

Thank goodness my conscience was healthy and awake enough to help me put this behavior in check. I finally realized this was missing in the world and my immediate environment. People were not setting a high standard of integrity for their lives and actions, and it was screwing up the world and influencing my behavior. I wasn't happy about that at all! I didn't want my actions to contribute to the madness! I knew I wanted to be the best person I could be, regardless of what the rest of the world was doing. I began to understand that the only way for the world to not destroy itself was for people to believe strongly in themselves and their abilities. Low self-esteem is the root of failure.

Now, let's look into some of the signs that show up when you don't believe in yourself:

- **You become lazy:** The moment we start doubting our abilities is when laziness sets in. We feel relaxed when we don’t accomplish a set task and are just fine, rather than working on ourselves to gain new skills and abilities to help overcome our obstacles.
- **You stop trying:** We either don't start on the goals we have set for ourselves, or we start and quit halfway through the moment we stop believing in our abilities and what we can set out to achieve.

- **You lose the lust for life:** At this point, your sole aim is to survive rather than live and thrive. You've already lost that zeal to excel. You do things to make those around you feel like you're trying when that isn't true.

- **People stop believing in you:** We all have expectations, and most times, people tend to develop good faith in us, thinking we can do remarkable things. However, their trust in us fails when we don't perform as expected. That's why you must believe in yourself before others can do the same.

- **You make up excuses and blame others:** This is the easiest thing to do—make excuses and blame others for your woes. We come up with vague reasons that logically make no sense instead of putting in the effort to get things right.

Why Do You Struggle to Believe in Yourself?

When we doubt ourselves, one of the most common reasons others believe in us is the most obvious. Public speaking, the biggest fear of most people, is one good example.

Think about the last time you were asked to get up before a group of people and talk to them. It was a scary experience. I address thousands of people every year, so I'm not afraid of speaking in front of groups, whether small or large. Why is that? It's because I believe in myself.

Psychologists have studied this deeply. They found that some people are not afraid to speak in front of others because they believe in themselves what they want to say and are confident that they can get up there and do what needs to be done. On the other hand, people who are afraid of public speaking don't believe in themselves. They don't want to get up and say anything because they're worried someone might laugh at them for taking another side of an opinion—for saying something different from what everyone has heard. They're afraid their idea might be silly. They're worried their thesis might not work. I've found that many aspiring entrepreneurs lack confidence, too, yet confidence is the key to success.

I used to lack confidence and was extremely intimidated to speak in front of people. I felt, "Who wants to hear what I have to say? I only own a coffee-selling company in the middle of New York. Why do they care what I have to say? Look at people like Michael Dell of Dell Computers, who are worth several billion dollars. Let's listen to what he has to say. Let's listen to Bill Gates. What does he have to say? Let's listen to Joe Torre, world-champion New York Yankees manager. Let's listen to Elizabeth Dole, one of the brightest women alive. Let's listen to Phil Jackson, winner of six NBA world championships. No one wants to listen to Randy Wagner; he has a straightforward story."

That was what I thought the first time I spoke in public. I remember my first presentation like it was yesterday. I was asked to tell my story to a group of aspiring entrepreneurs. I was so nervous my heels were pulsating, and I felt like I was rocking back and forth, like one of those old-fashioned drinking bird toys. My mouth felt like someone had poured cement in it, and no matter how much water I drank, my tongue remained dry, and my voice cracked like I was going through puberty again. I was sweating profusely. But as I got started and went along, the audience laughed—with me, not at me. During my talk, an African-American man in the front row said, "awesome," several times. He must have been a genius because he gave me the confidence I needed. My tongue suddenly became normal; I stopped shaking.

Strong self-belief and high self-esteem are essential because they help us move forward. Understanding this allows you to make critical changes to your lifestyle and become the best version of yourself.

While many do not want to think that their past impacts their future, it can. The people who believe in us come from backgrounds and relationships where they were admired for their successes.

This could be someone whose background and relationships are similar to yours, but they had someone who saw something in them and helped them become successful.

What Happens When You Believe in Yourself?

You are and will become what you think about. Why don't we ponder on that for a second? That means if you think you're going to succeed, you will. If you believe that you're going to fail, you also will. This boils down to positive thinking. Self-confidence is critical to your success. Without it, you'll never make it. So, use positive thinking to help you reach your goal. The body works better when the brain is full of positive thoughts.

The moment you start believing in yourself and your abilities is when you begin to attract miracles, become less judgmental, handle criticism more objectively, and increase your power of persistence. At this point, your potential for success will become exponential, and you'll inspire others to believe in you.

Positive people usually succeed because they want to see the good and ignore the bad. Optimistic people also lift everyone around them. Your team will catch on and feel better about themselves if you are positive! They will run through a wall to you and elevate their performances to their utmost potential.

How to Trust Yourself

Maybe there will always be people with low mentality and character on this planet, but I'm not one of them! Making this clear choice for my life and actions gave me strength, peace, and joy and helped me believe in myself more.

Some people's self-esteem is entirely driven by their desire to own material things and control others; you can see how that has screwed up this world! I knew I had made the right choice for the right reasons, and I was determined not to be pulled in by the dark foolishness that often takes place on this planet. So here are the tricks I use to make the job easier:

Block out undesirable events, people, and energy: As I became more aware of the sinister possibilities of every culture, I understood how important it is to define a clear set of principles to live my life by. And I knew that to maintain that high standard of life, I had to block out undesirable events, people, and energy. All successful people do this! Realizing that the world is full of unsavory temptations, people, and choices, successful people never allow these things to lure or affect them emotionally. They jump over hurdles, block out nonsense, and live a fulfilled life by building integrity and a desire to contribute to the health of our planet rather than the chaos.

Trust your decision-making abilities: We are all born with a strong belief in ourselves. But then life, people, and situations trample all over our passion and spirit. People try to throw different suggestions at us and perhaps say something cruel or judgmental, and our inner joy and confidence fade a bit more. Next, we get frustrated with the injustice we see and let it dwindle our inner light. This is why you must learn to be confident in your decision-making abilities at all times so it can let goodness filter in and keep harshness blocked out. This applies to your business and your personal life; you must learn to trust your decision-making abilities to allow your light to shine through.

Promise yourself to be your best: Believe in yourself because you are part of this vast and fascinating universe. Isn't that reason enough to feel special and feel like you matter? Like everyone else, I sometimes get tangled up in the hustle-bustle of everyday life and temporarily lose sight of the natural miracles around me. But then I slowly draw my awareness back to my appreciation for our lives' tremendous beauty and wonder. I am struck with awe. Knowing I am a part of it all, I feel inspired to do my best again. Understanding your strengths and weaknesses will help you support yourself too, which could make it easier to trust your judgment.

Find ways to express yourself: People are often ignorant of their personalities and what matters most to them. Hence, it would help if you took the time to learn what unique ways you like to express yourself and let them be enough for now. If you only want to throw a ball against a wall, then do that. If doing that relaxes you and creates a comfortable rhythm within you, then let that be your starting point for getting to know yourself better. Let your belief in yourself free your mind to do whatever brings you joy so your confidence and talents can gradually surface. Have faith that you have a right to partake in life's mystery.

Think of the things you have already accomplished: Believing in yourself can also be strengthened by remembering the small things you've accomplished, like riding a bike. Every time you got on that bike, it got easier to handle, and your confidence grew. So it is with any goal. You're uncomfortable the first time you try something new until you've had some practice at it. Find the willpower to try new things so your self-esteem will grow stronger daily.

Harnessing the Power of Self-Belief

You need to acknowledge that the power of belief is a significant driving force, and for you to harness this power, you need to do the following:

Think of success, not of failure: Thinking of success conditions your mind to create successful plans. Thinking of failure does the opposite—it prepares the mind to think of other thoughts that produce a loss.

Remind yourself regularly that you are the best version of yourself: Successful people are not supermen. Success does not require super intellect, nor is it based on luck. There is nothing mystical about success. Successful people are just ordinary folks who have developed a belief in themselves and what they do. Never—yes, never—sell yourself short.

Believe big: The size of your belief determines the size of your success. You should expect little achievements when you think of achieving little goals. However, you can expect significant success when you think of big dreams.

Action Points

Before proceeding to the next chapter, reflect on your life momentarily. On a sheet of paper (or several sheets), you should write the following:

1. At least three times, you've lost faith in your abilities and suffered their negative impact on your life. Writing them down will help you deal with them.

____

____

____

2. At least three ways you can follow to trust yourself better. You can make use of the"How to Trust Yourself" section to come up with ideas.

____

____

____

3. A mantra that reminds you that you are important and enough. This may include those people, events, possessions, and accomplishments you have been most pleased with. Take your time and enjoy making this list. You also might want to include compliments that you have received from others.

____

____

____

____

"The moment you put a deadline on your dream, it becomes a goal."– Harsha Bhogle

---

CHAPTER TWO

Change How You Set Goals

We often can't visualize ourselves achieving something until we accept the responsibility for getting it. The real failures are those who do not accept responsibility for their lives and blame others for their losses. Many will testify, "I am a self-made success!" However, few of us have heard someone say, "I am a self-made bum!" Yes, we want credit for our successes but not for our failures.

Once we accept responsibility and set goals, we are on our way to better lives. We can't control everything that happens to us, both the good and the bad. But we can control how we respond to whatever happens to us. Our responses ultimately determine what our lots in life will be. I know many people who have faced the most remarkable tragedies, yet they are among the happiest people I know.

On the other hand, I also know those who have had everything handed to them on a silver platter; still, they are among the most miserable people on the earth. Now you can learn something from this.

1985, I graduated from college and started supplying coffee to private and public organizations to create an extra income source. I'd been working only a few months when, one day, I found myself discussing the subject of change with Mark Brown, one of the company's managers. It seemed he wanted me to make some changes for the better. I informed him that I was already planning to make these changes.

I will never forget that Mark said: “Randy, people change, but they don't change very much, and they don't change very often.” I believe that statement bears repeating even now. Let's study it together for a moment.

What do you think of that statement?

Do you agree or disagree?

How would you respond if your boss said that to you?

Without wasting time analyzing what he said, I quickly replied, “Mark, I don't care about what people do or don't do. I am Randy Wagner, and I will make a change.” I know that might sound arrogant to you and maybe him too. But I've had the time to evaluate his statement, which I've found very accurate. It is so true that sometimes it's downright painful. Observing myself and others over the years, I realized that recognizable changes rarely occur. Incidentally, I did make the necessary changes. However, I’ll admit that achieving those changes was probably more accessible and confident because of my desire to prove Mark wrong.

Although it might be true that change doesn't come quickly and people don't change very often. But that doesn't mean we cannot change if we are determined to change. It might take determination and effort, but is it worth it? That depends on the change that we're considering.

What's Wrong with How You Set Goals?

Why do most people fail to establish goals for themselves? Let's examine some popular reasons:

- **Not realizing "why":** We aren't likely to do something stressful if we don't think it's necessary or valuable. Goal-setting takes work. This work, however, has tremendous benefits.

- **Lack of knowledge:** Goal-setting is not a skill we're born with. We must learn it. We've often tried setting goals, only to fall flat on our faces, and we decide never to try again. We put our goals the wrong way, and this works against us instead of for us. Most of us won't try to work on expensive equipment if we think it is too complicated. Also, we will not spend much time setting goals if we know how. Not knowing something is not shameful. The only shame is in refusing to learn something crucial to our future. If you don't know how to set goals, you should make it your first goal to learn how!

- **Fear of failure:** Fear of failure keeps us from setting goals. We see failure as something to avoid at all costs. Perhaps people had laughed at us before when we failed; we don't want to experience that again. Interestingly, the fear of failure usually brings about the failure you fear the most. Think about it—if you're going to do something and fail to try because you might fail, the result will be the same. There are many ways to become an actual failure, but never taking a chance is the surest.

- **Setting vague, non-specific goals:** Our goals should be determined by our purpose in life. The reverse is usually the case since most people can't tell their purpose from their dreams. Their goals give them meaning. You cannot be anything if you want to be everything. There is only so much that you can do. You can't please everybody; if you try, you probably won't please anybody—not even yourself! Unless you find your purpose and direction based on your goals, you will constantly wander around, doing little.

- **Lack of confidence:** When we have little or no faith, we will try to accomplish very little. And, since we tend to get what we expect from life, we'll get tiny. If we expect very little from ourselves, we won't be disappointed. An adage that bears repeating is, if you think you can, you're right. If you feel you can't, then you're right as well.

- **Poor self-image:** A poor self-image might be the main reason you don't set goals. You don't feel you deserve the fulfillment of our desires. Self-image refers to the way you see yourself. You cannot consistently act inconsistent with how you see yourself. If your mental picture of yourself is one of failing, you most assuredly will fail. Your self-image works through your subconscious mind to help or prevent you from doing anything inconsistent with itself. It also tries to convince you that you don't deserve some things incompatible with the way you see yourself. Many things can be done to improve our self-image. The most significant boost to my self-image occurred when I forgave myself for my failures and mistakes and appreciated my creative ideas. Other ways to improve your self-image include accepting what can't be changed and improving what can, committing yourself to a great cause, always dressing and looking your best, not comparing yourself to others, etc.

- **Underestimating time and distractions:** Time is precious, so it makes sense that we must make the most of our time. I'm lucky I learned to enjoy working at an early age. Perhaps it was the benefits (paycheck, praise, etc.), or maybe I sensed a fulfillment of purpose by working. Fighting laziness with good, old-fashioned hard work is more fun and productive.

- **Lack of discipline:** We must be disciplined to do those things that have not yet become habits or do not seem like fun. It takes discipline to begin an exercise program. It takes discipline to do what our bodies beg us to put off today until tomorrow. Sitting down and planning the rest of our lives is not necessarily something that must be done today; it can wait until tomorrow. Since it can wait, it probably will. As we all know, tomorrow never comes. We're all going to figure out goal-setting one of these days.

The 7 Dimensions of Goal Setting

Since a goal can be anything you want and are willing to strive to attain, it can also be anything you sincerely want to do, become, or have. Otherwise, it's only a dream or wishful thinking. This section will show seven major categories for setting goals for a balanced life. These categories are:

1. Social and personal development

Of the seven categories we will discuss, this is my weakest area. I stay busy almost every waking moment and find little time for personal activities. I must schedule time for it. People are either task-oriented or people-oriented. No doubt, I am task-oriented. If push comes to shove, I'm more concerned about accomplishing the task, even if that means hurting someone's feelings. For instance, I find it difficult to attend a social function and have a good time. I have a great time almost every waking moment anyway—in pursuing my goals. To quit what I'm doing to attend a function where people stand around talking is not my idea of a good time.

I've shared this with you in case you're like me. I don't believe you have to change your attitude to accomplish a lot. If you're like me, you probably feel you already have all the friends you have time for. The key now is making sure you take the time to keep those relationships alive. Aspire to help others enjoy themselves when they are with you. You can be an inspiration to them. I love life and believe the way to get the most out of life is to focus on giving—not on getting. So, I accomplish many of my personal goals by giving myself to others and helping them achieve their objectives or solve their problems.

2. Career and business

Most people think about careers when they think about goal-setting. Even high school students are asked if they've defined their career goals. Yet, sadly, very few define their goals.

Your career goals range from what you want to do to where you want to do it to how much you want to earn. They range from the education and skills you wish to attain to the type of people you wish to work with, the company you want to work for, or the business you want to set up. Your career goals might be awards and achievements to have to your credit, or it might be your attitude toward your job. You may wish to own your company or work for someone else. Career goals can be these and much more.

3. Finance

Indeed, this financial category is essential to each of us. Money significantly affects each of our lives. We must decide how we're going to:

- **Earn it:** Before you can do anything with your finances, you must have finances. Unless you inherit a bundle or win it, you must have income. There are two main categories of income: earned and unearned. Earned income refers to wages, salary, fees, or commissions for performing a specified service. Unearned income refers to money received from investments such as interest, property rent, and stock dividends. Begin by determining your current total income from all sources. Then, calculate what you expect it to be in the years to come if you continue on the same road you are currently traveling.

- **Save it:** Few things in life are more complex than saving money. Saving money is a discipline and not an easy one to build! However, we must discipline ourselves to have long-term, short-term, and emergency savings. Long-term savings are for retirement. I never expected to retire, but I know I might outlive my earning years. Second, short-range savings can be used in the next few months or years to buy items that cost more than one would typically maintain in his checking account, such as cars, vacations, property, home improvements, etc. Finally, emergency savings are money available when the unexpected expectedly occurs. Think about it. Isn't it foolish not to expect the unexpected? Though we can't always predict actual emergencies, we know they occur regularly. In every life, a little rain must fall. Emergency savings will help take the sting out of those situations.

- **Invest it:** Investments are financial ventures that can increase your wealth or bring in extra income (unearned income). Keep in mind that it's often possible to lose your investment! Two kinds of people should never gamble: those who can't afford to lose their money and those who can. Be sure you have as much information as possible before investing, and check out that information's reliability! Simply putting something in black and white doesn't make it accurate. Find out how much control you will have and the penalty for getting out before a deadline.

- **Spend it wisely:** I love this area of financial interest! I don't get excited about earning, saving, or investing, but I can get excited about spending it. I enjoy spending and mostly want to spend on fantastic deals. I'm convinced you can make your income go at least 50% further by planning carefully in this area. You can start by planning for purchases, not using your credit card for impulse buying, studying to sharpen your negotiating skills—at least read a book on impulse buying—and, perhaps, buying used items.

4. Family and relationships

We would probably all agree that family goals are essential. Most people say their family when asked to name the most crucial thing in their lives. How sad that we don't usually live like that! The family unit is the backbone of every nation. History shows that when a country's families collapse, so does the government.

As with anything, improvement must begin with you. You can't care about what happens to other families if you don't care what happens to your own. You might say you care about your family. You might even say they are more important than anything else. But if you're not willing to devote time *to* them, not just *to* them, your actions will speak louder than your words.

Look for ways to improve your relationship with your spouse, children, parents, siblings, in-laws, grandparents, grandchildren, cousins, uncles, and aunts. Indeed, some of these people mean more to you than others. Still, none of them would mean much if you don't let them know you care.

Decide how much your family means to you by analyzing the percentage of your goals directly related to them. Has your love for them reduced? Are arguments common in the house? Does your spouse seem uninterested in you or uninteresting to you? Are you respected at home? Well, don't expect changes until you're willing to change. Your family will eventually respond, but you must change first!

5. Health and wellness

You have come full circle on this wellness spiral, back to where you began—at choosing. Your initial choice, conscious or unconscious, was that you want to be well. Perhaps you have had a chronic health problem and have already made several unsuccessful attempts to change your health patterns. Or maybe you are suddenly faced with a new health crisis that has caused you to scramble to find answers. Notwithstanding the reason you are reading, it shows your commitment to regaining wellness and wholeness. In this step, you will transform your commitment to wellness into a concrete plan for improving one area of your health and learn how to support that plan.

6. Mental goals

Mental goals are essential. Nothing affects the way we live and the results of our lives as much as the material we put into our minds. Years ago, I heard Zig Ziglar say, "You can change what you are and where you are by changing what goes into your mind." That statement made sense then and has repeatedly proven itself to me.

The computer term "GI-GO" means "Garbage In, Garbage Out." If garbage is sent to a computer, debris will come out. The mind works the same way! We can't fill our minds with trash, hang around negative people, and spend our time worrying without it negatively affecting us. Remember Earl Nightingale's recording "The Strangest Secret"? His message was that we become what we think about most of the time.

7. Spiritual growth

Yes. all these and more are true! Yet it amazes me how few people take the time to give them much thought. I am often asked for examples of spiritual goals. Most people don't set spiritual goals; they also admit to being uninterested in them.

I am writing this book to share what I have learned, not preach to you. I am grateful I was introduced to this spiritual realm in my early days. I received God's forgiveness and was born into His family at a critical time. Before then, I had always thought God was off in the distance somewhere. I wasn't even sure He existed, let alone that He might love me. I was very lonely at times and often considered suicide. My spirit was troubled, and I had no peace of mind. I was looking for a purpose and unsure if I would find it. I probably wouldn't have if I had continued in the direction I was heading.

In case you haven't heard, eternal life is a gift, not something you must work for. You can't earn or qualify for it through your work, even if you tried. Over 150 times, the New Testament teaches that the way to obtain eternal life is to believe in (place your faith in, rely on, trust in, and put your confidence in) Jesus Christ. You can't have it if you're too proud to receive eternal life as a gift. It's as simple as that. Notice the simplicity in the following verses.

Each goal you set may be classified under one of these categories. Which category do most of your past goals come under? Which classes have you omitted entirely? The answers to these two questions explain why you are who you are today.

Setting Your Business Goals the Right Way

I must confess, I lived without a plan until I envisioned starting my coffee business when I discovered goal setting. Oh. I had dreams like everyone else, but I didn't know how they would become a reality. All I could do was hope they might someday. This section covers the different types of business goals and shows you how to set them appropriately.

The importance of our dreams will make us live life with purpose. Instead of hoping your dreams miraculously happen, you can achieve them through goal-setting.

The reason for this is simple. It is tough to do anything worthwhile without a clear direction. An action plan giving clear advice is necessary for a dream to become a goal. Once we have a clear path, we can focus our efforts and eliminate confusion.

- **Time-based goals**: Time-based goals can be further classified into long-term and short-term goals. While the former represents the overall direction of your business and how it will be in operation over the following months or years, the latter involves you breaking the long-term goals into small bits to be achievable in a shorter time frame.

- **Performance-based goals**: Performance-based goals are those you set to enable you to do specific tasks. They are straightforward to evaluate. Examples include how well your business products fulfill customers' needs or how your marketing campaign converts new leads into clients or customers.

- **Quantitative vs. qualitative goals** are number-based or statistics-based goals that can help you measure how well a branch or tool you use in business performs. One good example of a quantitative plan estimates how much sales your newly designed business website brings. The equivalent qualitative goal will be your customers' perception or thoughts toward the design and how well it engages and makes them take action.

- **Outcome- vs. process-oriented goals**: Outcome goals are those you look forward to achieving at the end of a task or set objectives, while process-oriented goals are those you stick to while carrying out your dreams. For example, your outcome goal could be to launch a new marketing campaign for your new product at the end of the month. In contrast, a process-oriented plan considers user experience, branding, content, etc.

Regardless of what type of goal you set out to achieve for your business, you want to stay true to the best goal-setting process—and that is setting SMART goals. If you search the internet for "SMART goals," you will get more than a million results. The term "SMART goals" has long been used by motivational speakers, exercise and fitness gurus, and corporate trainers and planners. The definitions of S-M-A-R-T vary, but most focus on specific, measurable, achievable goals within a particular time frame.

I have been teaching SMART goals to help entrepreneurs and business owners focus on improving results, not just functions. I began using the term "SMART" to describe the goal-setting process. I define the acronym as "Strategic and Specific,

Measurable, Attainable, Results-Based, and Time-bound," with each part of this definition being critical to business success.

Action Points

Now that you have come to realize what goal setting is all about, you must grab a sheet of paper and begin to write down the following:

1. What are your goals for all the seven dimensions of your life?

____

____

____

2. What goals are you looking to achieve with your business?

____

____

____

3. What mistakes have you been making when setting your goals, and what should you do to change them?

____

____

____

"Proximity is power. If you can get proximity with people that are the best in the world, things can happen because of all the people they know, their insights, and their life experience. They can save you a decade with one insight."-Tony Robbins

CHAPTER THREE

The Power of Proximity

Of all the secrets I'll reveal to you in this book, without question, none is more important than this one. It has made more men and women millionaires, myself included. And the secret is you surround yourself with winners, both at work and in your spare time. For starters, I've found that winners study other winners. They constantly search for new and better ways to do things and ask others for help. Now, this practice is what I call the proximity principle. Proximity is a powerful tool if you learn to use it well.

Think and Grow Rich by Napoleon Hill is a study commissioned by Andrew Carnegie. The author interviewed over 500 millionaires worldwide to find out what they had in common that might be responsible for their success. He interviewed people like Henry Ford of automobile fame; William Wrigley, Jr., chewing gum magnate; George Eastman of Eastman Kodak; Charles M. Schwab, King Gillette; John D. Rockefeller, Thomas Edison, Theodore Roosevelt; Wilbur Wright (from Dayton, Ohio), Woodrow Wilson, William Howard Taft; Dr. Alexander Graham Bell, the inventor of the telephone, John H Patterson, founder of National Cash Register Corporation; M. W. Woolworth, the retail genius, and U. S. Senator Jennings Randolph. These are a fraction of the hundreds of well-known Americans whose financial and otherwise achievements showed they knew how to succeed. What did Hill find out about how they achieved success?

They all realized that other successful people who have done what you want to do could help you become successful. Why reinvent the wheel when someone else can give it to you? You don't necessarily have to read a book, go to college, or spend years researching the secret. Please go out and ask other people what they've done and find out what makes them tick. That is the quickest and best way to succeed.

The Proximity Principle

Surrounding yourself with people playing the game at a higher level than you are will help you achieve your hopes and goals faster. Paul Allen, an American business magnate, computer programmer, and researcher, is one of the best examples of the power of surrounding yourself with winners.

In 1975, *Popular Electronics* featured Ed Roberts on the cover of their magazine. Who is Ed Roberts, you ask? Today, he is a doctor specializing in internal medicine in rural Georgia. He also invented the first personal computer—the MITS Altair 8800. 1974 Roberts was busy trying to get this computer idea off the ground. He couldn't find anyone who thought it was a good idea for quite a while. Guess who rushed to Dr. Roberts's home in Albuquerque, New Mexico? Paul Allen did. At the time, Paul Allen was Bill Gates's partner. Part of what Paul learned from Ed Roberts helped him get Microsoft off the ground.

In an *Inc.* interview, Roberts said how he inadvertently helped launch Microsoft. He had spread the word that he would award a contract to the first person to bring him BASIC programming language for the Altair. "The first person who showed up was Paul Allen, and I hired him," Roberts recalls. "Paul impressed me then and still impresses me. I didn't meet Bill Gates for another six or seven months." Can you believe that? No one bothered to listen or to seek out Mr. Roberts. He was a winner, and he still is.

Once you've identified some winners, you must dig deep and almost pry into their past. These winners are winners for a reason. Study what they did before they became winners. This will lend insight into what you need to do on your path to success. Take Clay Mathile, for example. He didn't wake up one day and become successful. He took a long, systematic approach to success.

Surrounding yourself with individuals already successful in that area, whether in business, health, finances, or relationships, helps you model what has been proven to work, allowing you to compress decades into days.

Using the Power of Proximity to Boost Your Career or Business

Whether growing your business, career, or relationship, you should pay attention to the psychological concept of the power of proximity.

For instance, I'm always looking for winners to spend time with. If I meet someone at a chamber function, political fundraiser, party, or other gathering, I send them a handwritten note with some information about my company. If the person impressed me during our meeting, I would say in my letter that I'd like to have breakfast or lunch with them. A few weeks later, I would call them personally and ask if I could have breakfast or lunch with them. (I have to eat, so I might as well make it productive.) The $15 or $20 I spend on breakfast or lunch is one of my best investments. It has helped me build one of the most impressive networks of friends and winners. This network has taught me a ton and generated millions of dollars of opportunities.

Without question, this little secret has boosted my skills as an entrepreneur. The logic of surrounding yourself with winners is simple but sound, if not brilliant. Not only is it motivational to talk regularly with successful people, but it is also educational. Reaching the top won't be easy if you go through life and business without consulting others. Conferring with others will help you improve your skills and avoid costly mistakes. Sometimes, mind-boggling results can occur from seeking out, finding, and surrounding yourself with winners.

- **Look for "outside help," too**

You will never be the best if you only look for help inside your industry. It would help if you analyzed other businesses and people for ideas to get your venture off the ground. I have toured grocery stores, city government offices, tool and die shops, and car dealerships, to name a few. Many of my business's processes and systems come from other winning businesses. Business is business, as they say. The products and services may differ, but the goal is to make clients happy and make money.

- **Be a pirate!**

In my talks, I often describe myself as one of the world's greatest pirates. I then disclose how much money I've made by surrounding myself with winners and searching out new ideas. Don't be afraid to borrow, improve, and adapt ideas for use in your venture. Some pictures are copyrighted and thus cannot be legally copied. But most ideas and philosophies are up for grabs. People claim to be the creator of a process, an idea, a quote, or a joke. But few things like this can be traced back to someone specific. So, don't feel bad about copying someone's idea or process. If it's not legally protected, it's fair game.

Here are two examples: The ballpoint pen-inspired roll-on deodorant. FedEx's system for package delivery was inspired by the Federal Reserve's check-clearing process. Being an observant consumer has led to entrepreneurial fortunes in many other cases.

- **Find a mentor**

Now that I've given you an idea of how surrounding yourself with winners works, how can you do it?

You'll be instructed to find a mentor when you attend one of the business boot camps I host. You can rely on a business mentor for all types of advice. A mentor is a coach with skills or knowledge in an area you lack. Someone who has agreed to coach you in their area of expertise. I've had several mentors over the years.

- **Make a mastermind group**

"Mastermind groups" are groups that Napoleon Hill advised his readers to join by seeking out people who have goals and values of the same or greater quantity and quality as they have. Once this mastermind group is formed, you meet biweekly or monthly to talk about your progress toward achieving your goal, the idea being that every group member can help motivate and educate others to achieve their goals.

- **Share your success with others**

Most ideas we use for our business have their roots in another company or person. We have repeatedly taken pictures, improved, implemented, and shared them with others. Remember, do unto others as they've done to you. In other words, share your success and ideas with others. I've dedicated an entire two-and-a-half-day boot camp to sharing ideas! I brought in successful people from all industries to share their best practices, and all attendees were asked to share two ideas once they arrived at the camp.

Now that I'm growing my financial literacy and money management business, I've also sought out the leaders in that industry to talk with. We trade emails, notes, and ideas, and to your surprise, not mine, of course, as I'm very confident. I've rubbed elbows with some of the best in the industry. How? Just by asking. And you can do the same. Just ask for help. It is human nature to want to help.

Many heads working on an idea are better than one, and these are no ordinary heads! The more successful people you seek out, socialize with, and ask for feedback, the faster the ball gets rolling; the more quickly it rolls, the more pins it can knock down, and so on. So get your mastermind group and surround yourself with winners!

- **Build a network**

Now, you need to develop a network, and I'm not talking about the kind of network involving those computer cables that run through your office or house. I'm talking about that large group of people who fit neither the category of your friends nor your mastermind group but are just as important. Your network will help put your business or your endeavor into outer space. This is all the acquaintances, clients, colleagues, prospects, and others you know who can use the product or service you're offering or who know people who could use it.

Brian Tracy, a skilled speaker, author, consultant, and coach, teaches that anyone can become an expert on something in a year by reading everything available. If you read as Tracy suggests, search for info and companies in your niche, watch TV, and attend seminars, you'll get there in less than a year. I think you can do it in eight months. The knowledge you gain will give you confidence because, as we discussed earlier, knowledge is confidence, and trust enables people to conquer the world. Confident people succeed at a much higher rate than cowards. Look at professional athletes. Look how confident some of those guys are to return a punt in the Super Bowl for a touchdown like Desmond Howard did a few years ago.

There are several ways you can do this. Some are easy and cheap, some difficult, some expensive, and even fun. Here are some simple steps you can take to increase significantly who knows you:

- **Write articles or columns and submit them:** The second way you can draw attention to yourself and improve your network of people is to write articles or even a regular column for a local newspaper. It doesn't matter how big or small the paper is. Your picture and your name in print give you instant credibility.

- **Volunteer:** This means getting involved. You'll feel good because you're helping people, and you'll broaden your network. Any association you join should be an active member there. That's the only way you'll benefit. If I can't get involved, I won't join.

- **Be someone others want to be around**. Probably the most important way to network with people is to be positive. Approach people and be someone they want to be around. It's okay to be funny, but don't be too funny. It's okay to be interested in someone. Don't be over-interested. Smile when people look at you. Listen to people when they talk to you. Be positive (I know I mentioned positive two times), support others, and help them. Do these things, and others will help you.

- **Speak to groups:** Another way to create interest in yourself and network is to give talks. If you are a local real estate agent, talk to Optimist and Rotary clubs about the 10 things you can do to your house to get the best price for it on resale.

- **Teach:** Another way that you can network is to teach a class. If you own a local restaurant, it might make sense to teach a course in cooking. Sure, you may give away a couple of secrets, but you also might create significant interest in your restaurant just in the students you have in the class (and their friends and relatives). You may even find a few great new team members.

You can never have too many friends and acquaintances. It's impossible. Friends can help you in business and can help you when you need them. Remember that here, too, it's essential to target your efforts to people who can use your product or service. If you are trying to get a home remodeling business off the ground, mailing it to apartment owners makes no sense. Better to speak at the local Rotary club, where many attendees will be homeowners.

Action Points

1. Take a few minutes now and list three or four people you would like to meet for lunch or breakfast in your city. Sit and carefully analyze who you choose to spend your time with. Then, set up lunch or breakfast with each of them in the next two weeks.

2. Ensure that the goals of the people you plan to surround yourself with align with yours.

____

____

____

3. Try to write down a list of things you think you can do to improve your social circle.

____

____

____

4. Please go over the above list in the previous section again. None of these ideas cost much, so there should be no reason you can't do them.

____

____

"Silence isn't empty. It's full of answers."- Anonymous

CHAPTER FOUR

The Mind Hour

This right kind of thinking—deep thought—makes us uniquely human. This thinking is associated with new ideas that drive the world forward. This thinking ignites strategic planning, scientific discovery, and artistic invention. It is rigorous, focused, deliberate, considered, independent, original, imaginative, broad, comprehensive, calm, relaxed, attentive, contemplative, and reflective, where the flow of information is limited and the medium matters—what you might call "slow flow." It is not shallow, narrow, hurried, cursory, fractured, or distracted.

Observe some people sitting in front of a screen in their sanctuary. The chances are that they're not speaking but furiously tapping their keyboard. They seem to be in a hurry and, one suspects, aren't fully concentrating, waiting, as usual, for some new bit or byte of information to flash across the screen. An alarm on a cellphone wakes these people, and they often check the latest gossip on the same device before they get out of bed. They go out in a vehicle with screen-based information or an entertainment system and spend most of their day interacting with one kind of screen. They interact with their friends via screens in the evening and may finally sit down to relax on the internet. Sadly, these crazy habits contribute to the new dirty attitudes and behaviors we later contend with. In a world where people can escape from their phones, they rarely have time to think. And that is what we will look at in this chapter—you will unravel the importance of deep thinking and how to leverage it to advance your life.

However, before we can describe deep thinking, let's take a moment to consider the more general question: "What is thinking?" Thinking is a mental process that uses the mind, which involves directing it toward something—usually a sequence of ideas or statements. Thought, which is the content of thinking, usually occurs through words, but it is also possible to think using nonverbal elements such as symbols, images, sounds, or feelings. Nevertheless, for most of us, thinking is mainly verbal.

Rational thinking involves a sequence of ideas arranged in an organized, logical order. Each step follows the preceding one using the rules of logical inference. The first statement is usually called the hypothesis, and the last is the conclusion. For some people, rational thinking is the highest form of thinking, and all other ways are lacking.

However, the fact remains that there are other ways of using the mind, which are neither rational nor sequential; this is where deep thinking comes in. Most people don't know such thinking exists or are capable of it. The non-rational review would seem vague because we are used to identifying thought with rationality. An in-depth study is challenging to handle, not because it is complex, but because it is essential. Deep thinking is how the mind functions naturally, not something the reason must be forced into doing.

Compound Time

Abraham Lincoln once said,t “Give me six hours to chop down a tree, and I will spend the first four sharpening the axe.” It doesn't mean you are cutting down a tree; instead, it talks about the essence of setting aside the time to think and do some reflection, as that’s the easiest way to achieve any task.

Successful people do this often, which explains why they do well. Warren Buffet, for instance, once revealed that he spent more than 80% of his career reading, thinking, and reflecting. And that was how he became the CEO of one of the top 10 largest companies in the United States. Elon Musk, CEO of Tesla; Jeff Weiner, CEO of LinkedIn; Jack Dorset, CEO of Twitter; and Bill Gates, the founder of Microsoft, are good examples. While Jeff set aside two hours of uninterrupted thinking time daily from his daily schedule, Bill Gates has made it a habit to take a week off twice a year for deep reflections.

One problem with our communication-saturated environment is that the actual value of what gets exchanged can quickly become an afterthought. As the line separating the seriously consequential from the most entertaining blurs, shallowness sets itself as part of the human condition. Is it in the billions or trillions of workplace task interruptions that, on any given day, launch us into more or less furtive forays into the alluring realm of the digital? Do you need to recheck the BBC headlines, the silly video that just went viral, or the latest posts by your favorite news bloggers? Do you need to do it right now? How do those interruptions affect the quality of your performance within your company?

The first fundamental responsibility we have toward ourselves and others is choosing to think. Brent Patmos, founder and president of Perpetual Development, Inc., explains that he does thinking regularly—and, in fact, his entire focus as part of The Complete Leader faculty is helping leaders develop clear thinking skills. Brent describes clear thinking as "the ability to be self-aware so the leader can see things with greater mental and practical clarity."

So, in a sense, you need to intentionally devote more time to thinking to help you focus better and become an effective leader in your business and personal life. It will allow you to always think before you take any action. After all, leaders should be thoughtful, analytical, and reflective. But in an age of distraction, that is also our challenge. The first crucial step toward an engaged and meaningful life is bypassing the temptation to get distracted and amuse ourselves. The following section will show you how to make thinking time a part of your business culture.

Your Business Will Thank You

Now that you understand the benefits of setting aside time to think and how it can affect your business and personal life let's dive into how you can go on and make it a practical part of business culture.

Setting aside time to think about your business should be your way of life and attitude as an entrepreneur or businessperson. It requires putting yourself in a state of ageless growth and renewal by continuously gathering and thinking about new information to give to customers, employees, and suppliers. You give all these people what they want and need and get what you want and need in return. What could be more rewarding?

Running a business is about working hard and thinking hard in the information age. As a business professional, your craft should be making money with information and energy. You must have knowledge about management, marketing, and money. Find out more every day. It's the only way to stay ahead of the game.

Here's how to set aside a “thinking time” for your business:

- **Create a hard time to think:** One of the significant reasons many businesspersons and entrepreneurs fail to schedule a “thinking time” for their business is that they do not have it on their calendar in the first place. You might think you don't have enough time, but that is because you haven’t yet decided to designate a particular time for your thinking activity.

- **Write out a plan for your thinking time:** To succeed with your thinking time, you must write out an exact plan to follow. Using tools like Google Docs on your smartphone makes the process even simpler. You can write a summary of all the action steps you will need to take once you begin your thinking session.

- **Review:** You should try to review your previous thinking sessions and make notes ahead of your next session. That way, you'll have better insights to help you make important decisions for your business.

The bottom line is once you realize that constantly gathering, thinking about, and using information is the fuel for your business decisions, the key to keeping your customers, employees, and suppliers happy, and the source of your financial and personal independence, you will naturally carry on the process every waking hour. Time, as you know it, will become meaningless.

Your mind has no punch clock. It doesn't turn on at nine and turns off at five. Even family vacations will become refreshing opportunities to gather and think about information. You will always return home renewed and brimming with new ideas.

Information is limitless. There's always more of it, and it's constantly changing. You will eat, breathe, and sleep to keep up with it. Always think about how to gather more of it and use it to gain experience and knowledge.

Too Busy? You Can Carve Time for the "Mind Hour"

"I have no time," we say, but we always do. We lack the will and wisdom to commit our time to goals that would be smart of us to pursue. If motivated to do something, you will make time for it. I am not arguing that you are not busy. Most of us are. I urge you to consider that you are only as active as you let yourself be.

Now, you need to understand that there is only one source of thinking time: the time we spend doing something else. Go ahead without looking back once you identify the things you usually do but wish to stop to manage your time. Read on to discover the proven methods you can follow to carve time for your "Mind Hour":

- **Make thinking part of your way of life:** Although there is no substitute for the thinking we do alone, making thinking part of your way of life is not forgetting dialogue. I am talking about a genuine conversation that is productive because two people bring their knowledge and wisdom to the table in the spirit of sincere cooperation. Dialogue is beneficial in the first phase of a project when you do not know anything about it except for an idea, and at the end, when you think you know everything. You might turn "waiting time" into "thinking time." Nobody likes to wait. It bores us. It frustrates us, and it makes us anxious. Now, if waiting were just an occasional turn-off, it would not be highly worth attention, but waiting is a constant presence in our lives. So what if we made it our ally instead of resisting waiting? What if we transformed it into a stress-free, stress-reducing, and fully lived time of personal choice? We need sanctuaries where we can hide from the frenzy of life today by slowing down to the pace of thinking. Reconceiving waiting can give us some of these sanctuaries. Granted, you may not find this an effortless shift, especially at first. Radical changes in mental disposition rarely click into place without effort. However, the rewards will make your effort worthwhile.

- **Establish a weekly or daily thinking routine:** Schedule your daily or weekly thinking time. You can start by including fifteen uninterrupted minutes of pure thinking in your schedule every weekday. Focus not only on the practical needs of the moment but also on big-picture issues. In fact, the more you are pressed by current concerns, the more distance you should put between you and them, if only for a short time. You might set your fifteen minutes at the beginning of your workday on Mondays and sandwich them between appointments on Wednesdays. What matters is that you consider this daily or weekly appointment.

- **Find and cherish your thinking stimuli:** Whether wallpapering your dining room or doing marketing research at work, take your time to find and love your thinking stimuli so you can do things right. We have no time to think because we repeatedly do whatever we have been working on. Yes. Being diligent will be more time-consuming than being shoddy. But a shoddy job is not a complete job.

- **Specify your top three thinking goals:** You can prioritize writing down at least three essential and thought-provoking business goals at the start of every week.

- **Feed your brain:** It's fun to explore what your brain can do and stretch it as far as possible. Just like it's essential to keep your body moving and flexing, it's also good to work on your mind to keep it in top shape. Some sure ways to supercharge your brain are reading at least 3-4 books monthly and eating new information, stories, etc.

You might think that none of this matters, but it does. We need to do a little less and feel a little more. We need to slow down—not all the time, but occasionally. We must stop confusing movement with progress and avoid the idea that all communication and decision-making must be done immediately. Deep thinking involves accessing these more primitive ways of using the mind.

Action Points

Now that you know the importance of setting aside a "thinking time" for your business and how it benefits you, why not schedule a time on your calendar right now?

1. It would be best to start by identifying a time within your weekly schedule to do deep thinking.

2. Review the top three outcomes of the week and use the result to create action steps for the following week.

3. It would help if you thought of new, innovative ideas to help your business grow during your thinking session.

4. If you have a team, do not hesitate to involve them when brainstorming.

"Half of the troubles of this life can be traced to saying yes too quickly and not saying no soon enough." - Josh Billings

---

CHAPTER FIVE

Year of Saying "No"

It's a short, simple word. Not hard to pronounce. So why is "no" sometimes the most complex word to get out of our mouths? Because "no" is also a mighty word. And like any powerful thing, it can help us or hurt us.

Consider the power you exercise just by saying the word "no." It can keep people from wasting valuable time. It can tell a client who asks for too many favors that it's time to stop taking advantage of you. It can save you money. "No" is an indispensable tool that helps preserve your time and energy for the things that are important to you.

But because it's such a powerful tool, "no" can also be dangerous and must be used skillfully. It can disappoint people you care about, hurt their feelings, or make them angry. You risk stirring up trouble or conflict whenever you decline an invitation or dismiss someone's request. When that happens, it can leave you feeling guilty.

It has become almost a cliche in our culture to say we're stressed out. This leaner, post-downsized era sees many working longer hours with less support. For entrepreneurs, there's the ongoing quest for more business time and the compelling need to stay close to the employees in an increasingly complex and toxic environment. As the backdrop for our rushed lives, we're prone to information overload and constant commercial assaults from morning to night. We are confronted daily by severe, petty forces that consume our time, reduce our resources, and add noise and clutter to our lives.

We feel exploited and oppressed because there's never enough time for the things we want to do. We go through our busy routines—work, school, kids, household obligations, outside commitments—and wonder why life feels so unsatisfying.

We can turn to hundreds of good books for advice on managing our time better, getting more organized, and setting up all kinds of systems at home and on the job. Some sources are happy to tell us how to hurry up and do things faster, but there is another way to cope with this busyness. Instead of revving our lives to cram in more, we could slow down and eliminate some clutter and clatter.

This book section is based on the assumption that by developing the art of saying no, we can reduce the unsatisfying busyness in our lives, creating time and space for more fulfilling business pursuits. Focusing on the personal and interpersonal skills crucial to working successfully with customers, colleagues, subordinates, and supervisors, this chapter mines and refines the nuggets of essential business know-how: the time-tested truths and savvy from the cutting-edge. You wouldn't want to miss this chapter, especially if you run a business that doesn't always need saying yes. It's about making yourself heard and getting your way—without turning off your customers, employees, vendors, colleagues, and investors.

The To-Don't List

Anyone can make a to-do list, but innovative entrepreneurs make and follow a list of things they should never do. The more precise you are about what is important to you and the steps you should take to reach them, the easier it is to say "no." Without this, you may be less selective in the things you let distract you. I don't recommend inflexibility; quite the opposite. Knowing what is essential gives you more choices about whether to say "yes" or "no." Here are some of the reasons saying "no" is just as important as saying "yes" in your business:

- **Keep the clutter out:** It is easy to be distracted from or lose track of the big picture. Caught up in the moment, living for the day, following your emotions. Thinking and paying attention to things don't matter. To be successful, learning to say "no" allows you to stay focused on your ultimate business goals.
- **Don't dilute yourself:** Consider an ordinary everyday activity most of us do, like driving to school, to the mall,

to work, to the movies, to sports events, etc. The big picture is to get from one point to another safely. To lose sight of this is to be so distracted by something or someone else that you fail to return safely to your destination. This is the same as when you always say yes, distracting yourself with trivial stuff and putting yourself and others at risk.

- **Seek help:** To be an entrepreneur, you must have excellent self-motivation and the right people around you. Every day, things make you question your abilities and desire to continue. When faced with difficulties, I remind myself I haven’t come this far for nothing. Building a product from the ground up takes time and determination. Surround yourself with positive people who believe in you and your ability to achieve your dream and can offer you ideas for continuous improvement.

- **Think strategically:** Learning to think strategically is structured around three key questions: How do successful executives learn to think strategically? (Is it something they are taught? Where? By whom? How?) What successful executive strategists use learning approaches? What is essential to their learning to help them think strategically? Fortunately, learning the habit of saying “no” allows you to decide what you believe will contribute to the long-term success of your business.

Saying “no” in business will not just make you a more effective leader; it'll also help your business survive. If you are running a startup, for instance, having the ability to gracefully reject certain offers and ideas that won't benefit you at the moment can help your business stand the test of time.

When You Are Unsure . . .

As much as we hate rejection, we also hate rejecting. And most times, entrepreneurs say “yes” to avoid awkward situations. Faced with a potentially guilt-inducing situation, taking the path of least resistance is easier. While inside, we may be screaming, “No! Go away! Leave me alone!” on the outside, we summon a pleasant smile and say, “Okay!” If you are not sure of what to say, here are some of the things you can do:

- Ask for time to think to help you arrive at a valid conclusion before responding with an empathic “yes” or “no.”
- While thinking, you should carefully evaluate what both answers could cost you.
- Always listen to and trust your inner thoughts.
- It will help if you provide explanations for saying “no” so that you and the other party are on the same page.
- It would help to not sting yourself with rejection when giving “no” as your answer.
- Do not forget to pick the right place and time.

- Lastly, ensure you choose your words wisely to avoid misunderstanding or an outburst from the other party.

How and When Entrepreneurs Can Say "No"

This is a complex world, and one of the things we eventually have to learn as an entrepreneur is the art of saying no. Saying no won't make you the most unpopular person in your organization, and having someone say no to you doesn't mean that you are unloved or unwanted. If you think about it, you would probably realize that what is behind another person's no is just about the same thing behind your no. Nothing lethal (unless it's one of those "No, absolutely not, get out of my life" cases). "I happen to be busy, but that doesn't mean you aren't amazing," is almost all most no's are about. So, as an entrepreneur who is always looking for new ways to make money, here's when and how you should say "no":

- **When "yes" means losing direction or control,** While you might be hungry for success, you shouldn't be tempted to say "yes" to every opportunity thrown at you. Doing so means you won't be sticking to the goals you've laid down for your business. Hence, it would help if you learned to say "no" to specific opportunities.

- **When "yes" is a FOMO response,** Having a fear of missing out (FOMO) is what many business persons experiencc when they say no to an opportunity. We start to feel like we have just missed out on a fantastic or lucrative venture, and it now feels like a big mistake. However, when such a situation occurs, you should remind yourself that there will surely be more opportunities to exploit.

- **When “no” means winning a better deal:** In this case, you can say “no” to negotiate and win even more significant discounts, get better invites, and make more money. Saying “yes” to all the opportunities you see today will only keep you so occupied that you won't be able to win a bigger, better deal. So why not just win big?

- **If “yes” results in burnout:** “No” does not mean loss. Think of “no” as a way to redirect time and energy to truly focus and succeed in your core business mission. Remember that there are only 24 hours in a day. People are not infinitely productive. Say “no” to prevent burnout and relapse before you reach your goal.

- **Say “no” to improve your work environment**: When you say “no” to someone, you are psychologically unavailable to those looking for something, and you can confidently say “no.” Explaining the reason strengthens your position and satisfies others with explanations they are unlikely to discuss.

The most crucial thing in saying "no" is to be firm and caring. Few are offended by a polite refusal when it's based squarely on genuine empathy with the inquirer and an honest and open declaration of your position. If the interruption you reject is based on organizational or personal concerns, making an early appointment to discuss the matter is always appropriate.

Accepting a task or conversation of no value often involves resentment of the intrusion you have allowed. This is always reflected in your colleague or customer in several non-verbal ways. A firm, caring "no" will do less damage than a much-resented "yes."

You gain more respect through honest, open firmness. Trying not to hurt other people's feelings or working under the misconception that you must be accessible to everyone to be an effective manager or leader is far from productive. An effective leader manages time well and achieves this based on a healthy respect for the dignity of the people they relate to.

Action Points

Becoming more effective and achieving more in time is rarely a matter of making dramatic, incremental changes. Part of this is your constant awareness of how you say "no" to specific requests. So what you want to do is:

1. Identify when you should have said "no" but didn't.

2. Write down what you experienced when you said "yes" instead of "no."

3. With your results, make your to-do list.

"Fear keeps us focused on the past or worried about the future. If we acknowledge our fear, we can realize that we are now okay. Right now, today, we are still alive, and our bodies are working marvelously. Our eyes can still see the beautiful sky. Our ears can still hear the voices of our loved ones."

-Thich Nhat Hanh

CHAPTER SIX

Face Your Fright

Fear is a complex, largely involuntary chain of biological, cognitive (mental), and behavioral reactions that serves an essential purpose: to protect one from danger. It arises from many sources. For many people, several sources must coincide for the fear to develop—genes, temperament, learning experiences, or a combination. And speaking of genes, it is evident that fears and anxiety-related problems run in families. If you have one or more close biological relatives with an anxiety disorder, you are more likely to have an anxiety disorder yourself. Chances are, you don't inherit fear itself; instead, you inherit a set of biological characteristics (such as particular brain processes or sensitivity of the sympathetic nervous system) that make it easier for fears to develop. Beyond whatever genetic or physical elements present that set the stage for fear development, anxiety can be learned in some ways and defeated too.

Facing fears is serious business. It's time-consuming and at least slightly anxiety-provoking. So why do it? The short answer is that fear, and its variants (many of which are called anxiety disorders) are painful and impairing—so potentially devastating that many people decide to do whatever it takes to get them under control. Think carefully about why you want or need to beat fears. Suppose you're like most people with anxiety disorders. When you reflect on your situation, you'll find the motivation to sustain you through this challenging but advantageous self-help approach I'll show you.

A self-help approach can be a powerful and effective way to overcome your fears. However, seeing a professional therapist is undoubtedly an excellent way to go. As a business professional, the power to beat fears will be within your grasp if you follow the steps outlined in this chapter. If you need more help with that, these methods will get you off to a good start, and I have also shared a resource you can use to find a professional who can further help you. The method of beating fear as an entrepreneur I discuss in this chapter emphasizes figuring out what causes fear to persist daily. So, even if you don't know what's causing your worries, you can still create a good recovery plan and defeat them.

Is Fear a Bad Thing?

Billie had had a long week. He was busy at work; his mother was sick, and they were still unpacking from the house move a month ago. He didn't like coming home to a messy house. It made him angry. It wasn't just that he couldn't hang up his coat because the cupboard was full of boxes or he had to step over the piles of toys in the living room. There was something about the clutter that made him feel irritable. His wife worked full-time, too, and he knew she struggled to cope with the house and the kids. They'd already had one argument this week, and he couldn't face another. He decided to have a drink to settle his nerves. But instead of calming him down, the whisky and soda seemed to ignite his anxiety, sending him into a tailspin.

Many of us can relate to Billie's dilemma. As business people, our lives are often filled with pressures, deadlines, and the stress of managing many responsibilities, such as work and family. And those pressures can take a toll, leading us to feel a range of emotions, including anger, frustration, and depression, as well as anxiety and fear.

Certain situations can create an environment for fear to emerge, but some conditions can trigger it. For example, coping with a client's outrageous demands can create a situation that makes some people anxious. Still, when that situation is combined with triggers like a lack of sleep, the effect is like striking a match. Before you know it, your contract with the client has become painful, and arguments and those around you begin to wonder what went wrong.

Studies have shown that people who experience frequent symptoms of fear or anxiety are also more likely to be in poor health. They are also more likely to smoke, drink, and be overweight. While scientists have not yet discovered whether fear causes poor health or contributes to a fearful outlook, knowing that certain things can trigger feelings of anxiety can help you take control. Poor diet, lack of sleep, stress, work, and the negative thoughts in your mind can often turn an everyday situation into one that fills you with anxiety. Fortunately, these anxiety triggers are also parts of your life that you can change.

Healthy fears vs. unhealthy fears

The healthy use of our fears can protect us from danger and keep other people and things around us from getting hurt. The unhealthy use of our worries can impair our ability to function and paralyze us for no particular reason. For instance, you are afraid when you fail to stand up to a customer. You are so scared whenever you cannot ask that critical question from a group of people.

Unhealthy fear causes stress, sleeplessness, relationship problems, nausea, hot flashes, irregular breathing and heart rate, anxiety, and impaired social and work performance. Unhealthy fear causes isolation, prevents us from achieving our goals, and restricts and distorts our rational thinking patterns. Unhealthy fear promotes obsessive thoughts and compulsive behaviors and prevents us from being vulnerable in intimate relationships.

To avoid the unhealthy results of fear in our lives and business, we must practice continued self-awareness and evaluate and confront our fears as they arise. Because fear is such a powerful force, many react to their fears without ever testing their authenticity. If you drive at night and a dog runs in front of your car, you would respond with healthy fear by slamming on the brakes. If, in your mind, you only imagined a dog running out in front of the car (the same fear) and slammed on the brakes, it would be an unhealthy response because the threat or danger never really existed. The same is true of all aspects of our lives and business; just because we fear something doesn't mean there's any real threat or danger.

Paying attention when your body speaks

Just as fear creates an emotional response, it can also create a physical response. In the same way that we need to pay attention to how anxiety affects our feelings, it is vital to become aware of how it affects our bodies. Your thoughts, feelings, beliefs, and attitudes affect your body. Feelings of stress and anxiety, for example, can make your hands sweat and your heart beat too fast and, over time, raise your blood pressure. Likewise, how we behave physically, such as what we eat and how much we exercise, affects our thoughts, moods, and feelings.

Recognizing the signs of stress in your body means you can change your thoughts and focus to a more centered and relaxed mode, thereby reducing the stress and physical symptoms and improving your health and well-being.

Knowing who you are

Knowing who you are and what you need is essential to overcoming fear. Without a clear understanding of the kind of person you are and your needs, fear can quickly take over, filling in the gaps in your self-esteem with self-doubt and preventing you from fulfilling your potential. Knowing yourself well means taking control of your life and finding ways to get what you need, whether it's more friends, deeper relationships, or more time for yourself.

Entrepreneurs and Fear . . . the Facts

To an entrepreneur, doing is a term of art. It means starting, not quitting, and ultimately achieving some value that wasn't there before. Doing is the most valuable quantity there is. So why don't we?

We once did a survey where we asked over 100 people at random throughout writing this book whether they thought owning their own business, being their boss, launching a new enterprise, and creating jobs for others was a desirable goal. Most said yes.

But when we asked them, “So why do you think most people with the idea or the dream don't start their businesses?” they all answered with a one-word reply that starts with an F. They all said, "Fear."

And honestly, those people knew what they were talking about. When someone has something important they wish, want, or need to do—and they don’t—then some fear stops them. Whether they admit or even realize it, a small but insistent voice says to them, “I can't. I'm not strong enough. I don't have the power. I can see what's going to happen. I don't believe I can, and I don't like how this feels.” Underneath their anxiety, the person is feeling elements of more specific phobias or primary instincts, like fear of the unknown, fear of loss, fear of social isolation, or public humiliation, all of which trace back to the mother of all fears—the fear of death."

It is no different for entrepreneurs, who, at one point or another, are scared of losing big clients, managing the organization effectively, not running out of cash, and lots more. A U.S. Bureau of Labor Statistics study has shown that almost 75% of ventures fail within ten years, with fear of failure being a major contributing factor.

And even success provokes anxiety too. When asked whether he was ever afraid while building his multibillion-dollar business, Hamdi Ulukaya, the Turkish-born founder and CEO of Chobani (a yogurt company), revealed that he was always doing. “Because if I had failed, many lives would be affected by it,“ he explained.

But since the average entrepreneur is not a neuroscientist, that single word fear covers it all—and it accounts for the resulting lost possibilities, inaction, noncommitment, non-exploration, and non-starting for millions of people.

Yet, as you'll see, fear has a significant upside and a big emotional counterpart that can tame it. Turning these emotions to your advantage is the whole purpose of the next section. As an entrepreneur, knowing how to harness the power of fear and love can make you, your team, and your organization unstoppable. The force that results is belief— a point that trumps any idea, business plan, or graduate degree. No one escapes the influence of fear, love, and faith. When you understand how to apply them, you gain an extraordinary advantage for your enterprise—one that's impossible to overvalue in today's hyper-competitive world.

How to Get Unstuck and Fuel Your Success

The following steps will help you transform fears you may be experiencing in your life or business. The procedure uses written letters but can be practiced through imaging techniques. Because fear is a powerful, overwhelming, and paralyzing force, it might be better to practice it in writing. Then, once you become familiar with the principles, you can practice them in your imagination when an unhealthy fear arises.

- **Visualize yourself as unafraid:** Write a step-by-step script of events and role-play them in your mind and on paper. The last couple of paragraphs describe the feelings that accompany this scenario. Describe on the form how relieved, happy, peaceful, relaxed, and content you would be after that. It is essential to feel the emotions and write the thoughts so your subconscious can be reprogrammed with the new information.

- **Practice acting "as if":** Write a detailed description of the worst possible outcome of your fear. What's the worst thing that could happen? Once you write that down, put up the "as if" attitude—talk and act like you would if you were not scared or bothered about a particular issue. By writing a step-by-step script of events on paper, you will be better prepared to confront adverse outcomes and discover different ways to protect yourself.

- **The law of reversibility states,** “You act in a manner consistent with how you would feel in a certain way.” When you do so, you'll create a feeling consistent with your actions. One way to do this is by describing the best possible outcome of your fears. What would you like to happen in the future? How would you like to be treated? The best possible scenario is usually the exact opposite of whatever your fearful thoughts portray.

- **Confront your fears immediately:** Recognizing and acknowledging your concerns will be necessary. What are you afraid of? What scares you and causes anxiety in your life? Make a list of several fearful events and pinpoint the exact cause of your fear. Start this written exercise by explaining your worries and any circumstances accompanying them. Write down the environmental conditions and events surrounding the fearful events.

- **Move toward the fear:** Transforming fears often requires daily effort. Our fears are often built over a long period, and it might be necessary to repeat this letter exercise several times. The process will get easier every time you do it, and your fears will become smaller.

- **Deal with fear directly:** Imagine the situation that causes the anxiety. Allow yourself to experience the feelings that these thoughts create. Now, go ahead and confront your fears and work to get over them

Where to Get Professional Help

It doesn't matter what kind of fear you're facing; there is always a professional you can consult for help. Here are some of the sources you can try:

- You can get help from your general practitioner to develop a treatment plan.
- A psychologist.
- A trained counselor.
- An Anxiety Recovery Centre in your country.

Recognizing that you can say yes to what feels right and no to what feels wrong for you personally, regardless of what is right or wrong for others, is one of the most empowering things you can do. And soon, you will be filling up the dark spaces in your life with love and self-assurance, leaving no more room for fear.

Action Points

As you have read, you can eliminate fear by gradually exposing yourself to whatever you fear. Here are the action steps to follow:

1. You should list the things that trigger fear in you. Make sure you start small and safe.

2. Next, discover what scares you most about business.

3. Then try to find out how your fears affect what you do.

4. list things you can do to face life more fearlessly. It would help if you interacted with yourself every day until you felt confident and safe around those things you fear.

____

____

____

"Books are the plane, the train, and the road. They are the destination and the journey. They are home."-Anna Quindlen

---

CHAPTER SEVEN

Miracle Words

Books contain the knowledge of humanity accumulated over the ages. As Thomas Carlyle observed, "All that mankind has done, thought, gained or been: it is lying as in magic preservation in the pages of books." Books allow us to meet one-on-one with great thinkers, even if they are of a different locale or time.

More to the point, the books and articles you read daily will help you master and excel in business. Reading books not only increases our life skills and extends our knowledge as entrepreneurs, but it also goes much deeper. In many ways, reading determines how we think, which affects our imagination and thus has a powerful influence on the development of our emotional, moral, and linguistic intelligence and, therefore, on what kind of people we can be.

If we think of it as the formation of knowledge, reading has something to do with learning. Reading studies living reality, the reality we live in history, and the reality that creates us. It also turns out that reading a text without its context is impossible—establishing a relationship between discourse and the fact that forms the lesson. I believe this highlights what reading means.

Perhaps I can illustrate this by referring to the title of a book I wrote. In this book, I shared what makes successful people achieve their goals and how anyone can do the same. I revealed how entrepreneurs could create more time for themself and become more productive. But, above all, I showed the readers what the word "success" is and how to shift toward things that truly matter. The book is entitled *Habits for Success and*

Significance: 7 Secrets to Accomplish Whatever You Want in Business, Time Management, Mindset, Social Skills, and Entrepreneurship. No matter the level, age, or field of expertise of the people I teach, reading critically is fundamental. Reading involves critical perception, interpretation, and "rewriting" what is read.

Can a Book Change Your Life?

My life journey proves that reading the right book at the right time can dramatically change your life. Earlier, I shared with you how I started my career by creating additional sources of income by supplying coffee to private and public organizations. But before that time, I was earning a small income and didn't know what to do with my life. One day, my brother's friend—who noticed how I always complained and sensed potential in me that even I didn't recognize—handed me a copy of *The 80/20 Principle, Third Edition: The Secret to Achieving More with Less by Richard Koch*. It was the turning point of my life. Richard's book inspired me to quit my dead-end job and venture into business. The coffee business boosted my financial position immeasurably and has helped me become a successful entrepreneur ever since.

- **Reading can teach you lessons:** By all accounts, Abraham Lincoln was brilliant, but he was neither a genius nor a speed reader with a photographic memory. Instead, he took advantage of reading early in his life to transform himself into one of the most remarkable men in history through the incredible power of reading. In seeking first to read and understand, we accept that we are not the only ones with thoughts, feelings, and opinions and that other people around us might have ideas and concerns worthy of our time. Like so many different skills, most of us find that the more we practice reading, the better we will become at it.

- **It can improve your concentration and focus:** Challenge yourself to read daily to improve your concentration and focus; avoid the temptation of mindless TV shows. Do crossword puzzles, solve problems, memorize text, learn a language, plan a trip, design, budget, join workshops, plan your career, and listen to music.

  Reading gives you a different perspective on life: We discover our world, history, and ourselves. More than any other mental activity, assignment forces us to think, imagine, examine, grow, and, in the process, discover our world, our history, and ourselves. We can learn about people's entire life stories without ever meeting them by simply reading about them in a book. And when we read inspiring, thought-provoking books, we start to examine a shift in all phases of our lives. Reading can transform us from what we are right now to what we could be.

Why Entrepreneurs Need to Read

Of course, readers make better entrepreneurs. This is not surprising for us, who are committed to lifelong learning. However, many struggling business owners seem unaware that the book is their friend and business mentor. Equally shocking is that many small business bloggers and book authors prevent others from writing.

I once knew a disaffected entrepreneur who considered reading a waste of time. His travel nights were usually spent in the hotel bar rather than in a book club with books that might inspire or inform him. Instead, he tried to figure it out for himself. He made the journey unnecessarily tricky.

So why does regular reading matter so much when building a business? Here are some of the reasons:

- **It inspires you:** Many inspiring stories have been written by and about people who have gone from employees to entrepreneurs. Such stories not only inspire telling the tale of overcoming challenges; they are also vivid records of entrepreneurial thinking in action. By the way, fictional entrepreneurs can also help readers build an entrepreneurial mindset.

- **It boosts brain power:** "What I already know is enough" is not the mantra of the successful. Passion begets passion, of course, but keeping love alive is closely tied to staying curious. Books can keep you stretching, whether it's human behavior or building an online presence that catches your fancy. Reading books helps to stimulate and work out your brain, especially its language, which is responsible for vocabulary, communication, and spatial awareness.

- **It develops cognitive skills:** You don't need anyone to tell you that you live in changing times. Those who ignore the changes operate at a considerable disadvantage. As an entrepreneur, you want to have an active memory, strategically make decisions, and improve your verbal intelligence. Reading is scientifically proven to help you develop these cognitive skills. As Jim Trelease points out, "People who have stopped reading base their future decisions on what they used to know. If you don't read much, you don't know much. You're dangerous."

- **Reading helps you to speak better:** Reading can help you expand your vocabulary. The more you read well-written books, the better your speech will be, as you can build sentences and use words correctly. Observing how other authors write can influence your speaking at business meetings, conferences, and public speeches afterward.

Cultivating a Reading Culture for Success

If only we had a magic wand that could instantly transform any lazy reader into an avid reader, what a market such magic would create! But the realization that no such magic wand will ever exist is inevitable, as is the grudging wish that we knew more about the process by which we work slowly toward the end of entrepreneurs cultivate a reading culture for success and make use of the riches which are available to them in books and reading. However, no change is easy to achieve, and resistance to change often follows any effort to break away from old ways. So here are some ways you can cultivate a good reading culture:

- **Set a reading goal:** You are already goal-oriented; otherwise, you would not read this book. For your goals to be practical, they must be realistic and specific. Every exercise and reading from this point onward will have a clearly defined purpose: to help you learn how to speed read. It would help to list books you want to read, set particular times to read them, and choose a special reading corner.

- **Join a book club:** Book clubs and reading associations are another way to improve your reading habits. The main goal of these clubs and associations is to help speed up the book distribution system. They do so by encouraging the use of private collections of members, promoting contacts between publishers, book distribution centers, and libraries to improve the exchange of literature, and establishing museums of books and literature.

- **Get an overview of a book before reading it:** To get an overview of a new book, start by reading the front and back covers. Read the testimonials or the summary statement on the back cover. Read the author's biography to understand how his credentials relate to the topic. Open the book to the introductory pages and skim them. Has the author written other books on the subject? Who is the book dedicated to? Any special acknowledgments? Read the foreword, preface, and introduction. Take a few minutes to skim the table of contents. The contents page will give you a blueprint of the book and tell you how the author has chosen to unfold his arguments. Many readers skip these sections, thinking they're a waste of time. But they can give you valuable insights into the book's main points.

- **Make it pleasurable:** Reading is visually guided thinking. So, you want to read actively and make it enjoyable because active reading and "visually guided thinking" help you to gather information and increase your understanding. While you read, ask more and better questions—that is, more profound, more probing questions. This will reward you with a richer reading experience.

- **Attend book fairs and book weeks:** Book fairs, book weeks, library day, etc., are hosted in many countries worldwide. They may be organized on an international basis or at national or local levels through the efforts of volunteer groups, professional book associations, and the expertise of outside enterprises.

How to Pick the Next Book

Many people are faced with the dilemma of not knowing what to read next. The answer to the question, "What books should I read?" considers the whole world of letters and is so essential that no individual utterance, however sincere and competent, can entirely cover the ground. Different tastes and needs call for other suggestions. Here is a guide to help you pick the following books to read:

- **Consider your passions**: Passions are called passions for a reason. They are things that you genuinely love doing. Since you love doing them, why not read about them? You can't go wrong with reading a book about something you love.

- **Search the Internet:** Search for the best books related to your field. For example, if you love learning about marketing, you could search for the best books on marketing and sales. After your search, you will have many great options to choose from.

- **Think about the movies you like**: Movies and books go hand in hand. If you want mysteries, there is a good chance you will like mystery books. If you like business, search for books related to business, such as *The Wolf of Wall Street*. You can search for all these books on any search engine.

- **Take a trip to your local library:** If you would instead search in person, head to your local library and talk to the librarian. They will probably ask you questions and point you in the right direction to pick out books.

Reading is a hobby that starts when you are young, and as you age, it keeps you young. If you want to pick out books, the task can be simplified by following these ideas.

Action Points

Here's an exercise for you to do:

1. Make a list of books that you have read that changed your life

____
____
____

2. Make a short note of how you read and understood the ideas in those books.

____
____
____

3. list at least three books you'll read to help you and your business grow.

____

____

____

4. Now expand the note you created in step 2 by using what you've learned in this chapter to read your new books.

____

____

____

5. Reading together with a friend will be a plus.

Part II: Boss Moves

"For every minute spent organizing, an hour is earned."– Anonymous

CHAPTER EIGHT

A Day in the Life of an Entrepreneur

Being an entrepreneur has its excellent and crazy sides, often to the extreme of each. If you can turn your stumbling blocks into stepping stones, you are halfway to becoming a successful entrepreneur. Many start-up business books emphasize the mechanics of entrepreneurship: raising money, finding an idea, and marketing the concept. Sure, there are essential steps to learn, but before you worry about mechanics, you should steel yourself against the emotional ups and downs of the start-up world.

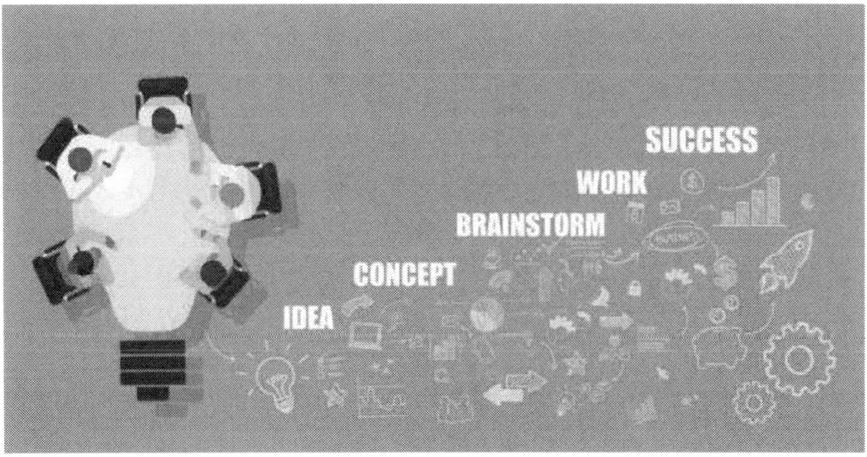

I developed a passion for financial literacy and money management from a young age, and I've always been keen on putting what I have learned into practice. Ever since I was a kid, I have felt so much joy whenever an idea, often in collaboration with others, gets everyone involved, excited, and motivated to work hard as part of a team.

My first recollection of this was when I was about 13, and my friend and I decided to set up a video club for students to watch movies after school hours. We raised enough money to buy a top-of-the-range computer for the school by selling fun-sized chocolates and cups of soft drinks. While in college, despite believing that I would become an entrepreneur one day, I became more influenced by the idea of working for a large and credible corporate company, such as a management consultancy or investment bank. I think this was partly because the careers counseling did very little to promote entrepreneurship as a career choice.

Over the years, I have maintained an entrepreneurial viewpoint in the back of my mind and tried out different business ideas while in college. These included organizing parties for the students' union and creating a company that uses interactive party games to break down social barriers. I then set up a small society to unite like-minded people interested in business and entrepreneurship. As a result, some of our members and I were invited to attend the entrepreneurship summer program hosted in our community. I felt privileged and motivated by my involvement in a program to train me to become a successful entrepreneur. Today, I have established several businesses, and my confidence has increased.

You probably have heard that more than half of all start-up businesses fail. My advice? Just ignore it! This may seem odd, but if you are frightened by a mere statistic, you wouldn't be able to do all the other things it takes to succeed as an entrepreneur. About half of all marriages fail, too, but that doesn't stop people from getting married or trying again after one marriage fails.

If you go into a business thinking that you'll fail because most people do, chances are, you will forget. It's that self-fulfilling prophecy thing. On the positive side, if you've got the right frame of mind and a solid plan, starting your own business can be the most satisfying and exhilarating experience. So, in this chapter, we will show you what a successful entrepreneur's routine looks like and how to organize your day for success.

Things Entrepreneurs Do Daily

Now, I want to share with you things entrepreneurs do daily. While I want you to go into it with your eyes open, I also want to encourage you with some of these things about being an entrepreneur. Starting a business as a first-time entrepreneur is one of those huge, life-altering events. As I explained earlier, it's like a marriage—running a successful business takes the same depth of commitment and desire. Like any relationship, if you want your business to succeed, you must work at it. So, let's talk about some of the things you need to do to succeed as an entrepreneur:

- **Visualize:** Entrepreneurs try to visualize what the future could be like for them and their businesses, and, more importantly, they can bring this vision to life. Most good entrepreneurs strongly desire to come up with ideas and products and develop something new. They want to be innovative and achieve big goals. They want to capture their dreams and visions in a concept. In many cases, ideas can push the boundaries set by society and industry and cannot be reinvented due to the long history of implementing them in a certain way. There, a paradigm shift can be very successful. Richard Branson is an excellent example of how anyone can transform their business, from music to airlines, mobile phones, and banking.

- **Establish a routine:** no single quality or trait is more important to being a successful entrepreneur. Having a way and being persistent about it makes you stay on track and keeps you motivated when things aren't going how you thought they would—and they rarely do. But I should add persistent determination, motivation, and belief.

- **Plan and act:** This trait sets apart those with dreams from those who succeed. It's great to dream, but then you must execute and turn the idea into a profitable reality. Once you believe in a statement, you must plan and act immediately to build momentum toward your goals.

- **Monitor progress**: It takes more than a simple amount of action to succeed; you need to monitor your progress and be dedicated to your plan. Monitoring your progress will take dedication, passion, and commitment. While dedication will help you meet the intense demands of running a business and drive you until you reach your goal, love is essential for entrepreneurs because, although rewarding, starting and building a new firm is demanding. Twelve-hour and seven-day weeks are common when an entrepreneur strives for a business. And, of course, staying committed means dedicating from a place of love. That love will drive and give you the energy to be saved when the going gets tough.

- **Exercise and meditate**: Most prosperous people and entrepreneurs take exercise and meditation seriously. Doing so helps them avoid defeat. Proper training and having quiet time for reflection will help you get things right when all else seems lost. Spending quality time with family helps entrepreneurs recharge too.

- **Communication**: These things discussed in this session would be useless without getting your message across to all the relevant parties. If you cannot inspire, enthuse, motivate, and excite people about your dreams, those dreams will be much harder to achieve. Excellent communication skills are essential to help you interact well with people of varying personalities and values, many of whom will not necessarily share your passion or motivation. You will need to talk your way out of the many roadblocks you will meet, from financing and legal issues to recruitment and simply helping people understand your idea.

How to Plan Your Calendar Like the Boss You Are

Time is relative. For those who are busy, it passes quickly; for those who are bored, it passes slowly. For the 15-year-old, time does not pass soon enough. For the 55-year-old, time is a little luxury.

For the entrepreneur, time is an irreplaceable resource. It must not be wasted. We each have only so much time. When it's gone, it's gone! Time is best used for business purposes to achieve primary goals and objectives.

To manage your time and plan your calendar like a boss, you will need to consider the following:

- **Schedule everything**: To manage your time effectively, you must systematically schedule everything you do and review it occasionally. The reviews should take place at least weekly. More often is better. Reviewing your goals achieves two essential advantages. It helps keep you on track and allows you to jot down any new ideas you've gotten since the last time you examined your goals. The review technique is a powerful tool. I have a binder-type notebook where I schedule activities and success-related information, including my list of plans and ideas. Every time I thumb through the binder,

I develop new ideas. I sometimes cross out ideas that have lost their importance.

- **Break down big tasks into simpler ones**: You should achieve specific tasks during your planning stage. You should review the items you wrote down on your note-taking device. You won't be able to do all the things on your list due to their complicated nature, so you want to break them into more straightforward tasks that you'll be able to do quickly.

- **Choose strategy over opportunities**: Here is an instance: the human mind can hold only one thought at a time. Sometimes, we try to think of more than one thing at a time, but it just doesn't work. From your experience, you know what it's like to get a powerful idea and then be confident you will remember it. What happens? A few minutes later, you're scratching your head and trying to remember that great idea. It would be best to have a strategy to capture those ideas as soon as you get them. All it takes is to write down a word or two. You can then go about your business with the confidence that your idea is in a safe place.

- **Eat that frog**: Wise time managers try as much as possible to avoid procrastination. Instead, they set aside a specific time each day to plan. Planning takes only a few minutes but can save you so much time. Some people prefer to do the craziest tasks first thing in the morning. For these folks, early morning hours are when their thinking is fresh and uncluttered. Morning planners are not necessarily "morning people." They find mornings are the best time for them to plan their day. It's a great time to think, design, and write books. Some people prefer to do the more significant task at the end of their day— the end of the workday or before they retire at night. When they go to bed at night, they like to know what they will do the next day.

- **Build unstructured time into your calendar**: Successful people have one thing in common. They concentrate their energy on activities that will help them achieve their goals. They give as much attention to the most minor enjoyable activities as to the fun ones. To guarantee your success, you must form the habit of planning each day's activities and then following through with your plan. It would be best to ensure that the less desirable tasks do not fall prey to procrastination.

- **Use the right tools**: I once heard someone say, "The shortest pencil is more reliable than the longest memory." It's the truth. You need to make use of the right tools. For instance, note-taking devices, such as a small writing pad or a 3x5 card tucked in your pocket at all times, are one of the most effective instruments for your success arsenal.

Action Points

Based on your learning of these entrepreneurial traits, you should write these questions in your book and answer them too:

1. How confident are you in bringing your conceived idea into reality?

____

____

____

2. What activities do you engage in daily that take a big chunk of your time?

____

____

____

3. Do you have a routine to help keep you on track?

____

____

____

4. How can you adjust your calendar to use your time efficiently?

___

___

___

Refer to the content of this chapter, and now think about the things you do and your ability to develop or work on areas in which you are less intense.

"A company's culture is the foundation for future innovation. An entrepreneur's job is to build the foundation."-Brian Chesky

---

CHAPTER NINE

Stay True to Your Brand

Strong company culture and true brand identity are essential to much troubling the business world today. Understanding those values—seeing them for what they are and what they do, where they come from, and how they interact with other competing values—can help entrepreneurs in specific ways.

Entrepreneurs faced many challenges in the late twentieth century. More critical issues are lagging productivity, burdensome social and regulatory costs, discontented and disloyal workforces, rising global competition, geopolitical turmoil, unreliable currency systems, episodic threats of inflation and recession, and general market instability. Deep knowledge of how an unbreakable brand culture urges entrepreneurs, workers, and firms to do what they do might help them survive present difficulties and ride the powerful social and technological currents transforming the world's business systems.

Creating an Unbreakable Brand Culture

Although it is difficult to establish a strong company culture and an authentic brand identity, these two values must come together in every organization, big or small, to form a solid basis for a successful long-term business strategy. These notions each serve a different purpose but create a driving force that allows for long-term and sustainable growth when combined.

Building an identity that will stand the test of time takes a lot of hard effort, time commitment, and patience, especially in today's ever-changing culture. And luckily for you, I have outlined the steps you need to follow to create an unbreakable brand culture for your business:

- **Define (your brand):** Branding is traditionally focused on goods and services. Coke cans, cars, and cashiers are all physical manifestations of the brand we see daily. But more and more brands are being separated from products and services. Now, they are competing for the space of the mind. For example, a virtual world in which channel branding is essential has emerged on the Internet. The great brands of tomorrow, decoupled from tangible goods and services, must place more value on consumers than ever. It is now necessary to define your brand to have a psychological feel. So, don't think about branding your current products and services. Instead, focus on cementing your brand in the hearts of your customers. The battle is about taking over and keeping a place in their imagination.

- **Write (your mission, vision, and values):** Developing a solid brand personality will help create a loyal brand culture. But this alone is not enough to guarantee the long-term success of your brand. Brands must also genuinely embrace the concepts behind relationship marketing. Brands must captivate consumers with their mission, vision, and values, just as hobbyists do. Once consumers have decided what they want, they should be content with what they want. Over time, they must build personal relationships, share beliefs, and seek mutual benefit.

- **Create (your identity)**: The shift to homogenizing products worldwide often shows that brands also need differentiation at the regional level. They need to create an identity for themselves. It is no longer enough for everyone to be everything. Brands need a strong personality. They need values and relationships. They need to attract strong and even fanatical supporters to be successful. Like pop groups have followers and fan clubs, brands need to develop an enthusiast base. This is only possible with clear brand differentiation. For anyone who loves a brand, others may hate it. The thing is, the fans are sticking with it.

– **Educate (your employees):** While brand culture between the consumer and business is desirable, a good relationship between the brand and the workforce is equally alluring. A brand is a perfect instrument for focusing the efforts of employees. Brands already have a clear identity and define their mission, vision, and values, so they must act as a guide to action within the enterprise (and are expected to operate outside it). This brand can be used to inspire employees. However, it should be noted that you cannot send messages inconsistent with your brand identity. Thus, brands play a role similar to corporate values, and companies articulate their values and use them to coordinate the activities of companies and their employees. In the case of a corporate brand, brand and corporate values are similar, if not the same. Companies that deal with product portfolios without a clear corporate identity find it more challenging to reconcile corporate value with brand value.

- **Get results:** Your brand needs to continually improve to survive. Innovation is the foundation for enhancing your brand. But brand innovation isn't limited to companies. There are even reasons why consumers should be involved in the process. Consumers will want to be part of a brand that has built a brand culture and loyal following.

Why You Should Stay True to Your Company's Culture

I recall when one of my clients had a low employee retention rate and came running to me for advice. So, together with my team, we analyzed their company, and that's when we realized that they hadn't been faithful to the values they presented. You see, my client's small firm had grown to become a huge corporation, thereby making it face increasing alienation among its workers. The challenge became how they would encourage high motivation and job commitment after the founder lost influence due to the increasing size of the firm.

Meanwhile, our experience working with different organizations has helped us know that most people working for large business firms often feel that their best talents are not used correctly in the workplace. Their perceptions are usually accurate. Those who do simple, repetitive tasks feel less involved with their work, less concerned for the quality of the product, and less responsible for their job. So, these employees felt like they had been duped and would prefer to leave. This alienation has been documented often over the decades.

Having detailed these issues, I provided my client with suggestions for providing greater involvement for the worker. These suggestions recognized the dignity of the individual worker and produced better results.

Now, talk about the benefits of sticking to your company's values. All companies need a values culture to attract the best people and compete effectively. People coming out of college today are looking for a company that reflects their values. The case can be made that companies that are the best in their categories consciously create cultures that make that success possible. Those cultures are based on positive values but are defined by and unique to each organization; there is no such thing as one-size-fits-all values.

Attitudes of your executive team members are just as important as employee attitudes if you want to become a company with solid and profit-enhancing values. If your executives' behavior does not reflect your company's values, no one will believe that values are essential. If one of your values is "caring," but you let a senior manager yell at employees, everyone will know that caring carries no weight in your organization.

All across the country, my team is helping companies use values and associated behaviors to deliver on their brand promises, create newer brand personalities, and make executing corporate strategies less of a Herculean struggle.

Staying True to Your Company's Culture While Scaling Your Brand

Growing your company is a positive thing. It shows that you are thriving and growing. It offers more potential to you and your growing team. It also implies you can provide additional services to your customers and clients. However, some companies forget to abide by their values when experiencing exponential growth. Here's how you can do it:

- **Create the environment:** A culture is the culmination of the leadership, values, language, people processes, rules, and other conditions, good or bad, present within the organization. The organization's leaders are instrumental in creating and directly influencing the environment. However, they cannot "create" culture, especially by assigning the task to a Culture Committee; they can only create the right conditions for it to arise. I recommend that you set up such committees, but you must realize that neither they nor the leaders themselves have complete control over what your culture will turn out to be. You can only create an environment to help your desired culture emerge and flourish.

- **Please do the right things the right way:** One of the best reasons for redefining corporate values is to help us make better decisions. And the front line is where most decisions about customer service should be made. In a company where customer service is one of its values, one of its behaviors could be empowering front-line people with tools and knowledge to handle problems personally and immediately.

- **Garbage in, garbage out:** Organizations will only reap what they are willing to invest in themselves. Values maintenance—continuous improvement—is as essential as value creation. In other words, you are never entirely "done" with culture; you must always be vigilant that no one backslides into old ways. This requires regular progress monitoring toward fully implementing the model and values-based leadership development and succession planning.

- **Build your company's culture on shared strategic values and financial responsibility:** These actions can set up the conditions for encouraging a culture that will make an organization a leader in its industry. It should almost go without saying that those values should also be vetted in responsible fiscal management. Happy-talk values that result in spending vast sums of money on questionable programs are not sustainable in the long run. But don't let financial concerns derail the process in its infancy. Counsel your financial people to give it a chance—it will likely save buckets of money sooner rather than later as turnover and training costs go down. It can even help companies avoid the high cost of a layoff—which will no longer be a first resort to cut costs —that has been shown to hurt stock prices anyway as investors avoid troubled companies.

Consider how your people would react if you asked them to step up and help the company thrive or survive. Would they sign on for shared sacrifice? Or would they look at your salary and perks and say, "You first"? Would they remember you hardly ever visit them and talk to them personally? Or would they recall how you've helped personally when things got rough?

When you are a company, division, or department leader, your actions matter, particularly those that display your values. Your people talk about everything you do, and it becomes a part of your company's DNA. The best leaders understand the incredible impact of their actions on how employees behave daily. Entrepreneurs are driven by competitiveness and performance. They want success for themselves and for the people they lead. They understand that long-term success is possible only when they inspire the people around them to come to work every day prepared to do their best.

Action Points

1. As a leader, list the values to which you will be committed and build a brand culture for your business.

____

____

____

2. Understanding that values drive organizational behaviors, you should define the values you've listed by behaviors your employees can recognize and emulate.

3. Note how you plan to create an environment that encourages a high-performance culture based on values.

"The heart and soul of a company is creativity and innovation." - Robert Iger

CHAPTER TEN

Find the Spark

There is probably no business subject where creativity isn't relevant. As an entrepreneur, you need creativity; even at the most challenging times, taking a step back from the action is essential. Creativity and innovation are words that you cannot avoid. Whether you listen to an arts program on the radio, a keynote speech at a business conference, or watch citizens urge their government to achieve more with less money, you will hear "creativity" and "innovation" being discussed. Yet creativity and innovation are classic examples of concepts everyone has a feel for, but few can describe. Arguably, there is a subtle difference between creativity and innovation. From the words' origins, innovation seems to be about newness, while creativity is about bringing something into being.

Harvard Business School's Theodore Levitt defined creativity as thinking up new things and innovation as doing new things, but this does not match the common usage of the words. Often, the invention applies to idea generation (perhaps because of its roots in "newness"), particularly around products, while creativity incorporates both innovation and the task of problem-solving. Of course, it is never that simple, as creative problem-solving is all about generating new ideas (to solve problems), and idea generation is simply solving the problem of getting a new idea (or product or whatever).

This chapter highlights the importance of creativity in businesses, how it works, and, most importantly, how you can implement it effectively for the benefit of your business.

Creativity Is Not Just for Artists

Usually, business and creativity are not discussed in the same context. A critical thinker in understanding invention, Arthur Koestler divides the creative process into three personas: the jester, the sage, and the artist. While the jester provides an aspect of creativity with which neither art nor business is genuinely comfortable, the sage has traditionally been the scientific and philosophical thinker, the picture of invention that has most influenced the industry, typified by the explosion of a new idea. The artist represents the traditional picture of creativity, whether composing music, writing, or working in the visual arts.

Both the arts and business take themselves very seriously, often to the extent of appearing sober. Yet humor is a powerful weapon for creativity. Koestler's persona here is very apt—the court jester was the only one who could question the monarch's decisions, but by doing it with humor, he made a practical point and avoided offending the monarch. A business that is to reap the benefits of creativity needs the humor of the jester to challenge the way things have always been done, the inspiration of the sage to come up with new products and services and to crack complex business problems, and the clarity of view of the artist to refine the ideas and ensure a good fit with the actual business. From a business viewpoint, all three of Koestler's persona are essential in defining creativity.

Many believe business is about making money, whereas creativity concerns art and imagination. In business, creativity is a way of thinking that inspires, challenges and assists people in finding innovative solutions and creating opportunities out of problems. It's why some businesses dazzle us with new and unique ideas while others tread water. It is a source of inspiration and innovation. Here's why creativity matters for companies:

- **It makes companies competitive:** Competition, growing customer expectations, global/local considerations, changing workforces, exploding information resources—a barrage of business problems and imperatives, each demanding a fresh idea. Change is ever-present and will not go away; it will get faster. There is no returning to the old days. If you can make your company innovative, you have the best chance of overcoming those business problems, coming up with great new products and services, countering the competition, and surprising your customers by exceeding their demands, not just meeting them.

- **It nurtures company culture:** In a company where creativity is not actively encouraged, the company culture suffers. Suppose creativity is accepted as a fundamental tenet of the company. In that case, the staff will do whatever is needed to get the job done, which is a whole different world from the traditional approach to work. Best of all, it is a win-win. The company does better, the customer is happier, and the employees get more out of their jobs.

- **It aids productivity:** If you can keep your company innovative—even more of a challenge—you can make new changes and boost productivity in a world of turmoil. This is a kind of productivity where difference is a constant, the stability of a gyroscope on a pitching platform, keeping the company on level while everything moves around it. The quote from Robert Iger at the start of this chapter is probably the least quoted extract from the American businessman. He is the executive chairman of The Walt Disney Company, yet the remark has never before been entirely so accurate.

- **It helps to solve problems:** Creativity is essential for any business. Creativity is the capacity to generate solutions to problems and value outputs. Without some such process, there is no obvious way to create and maintain a competitive advantage. For example, I might approach the problem of publishing a book by breaking it down to writing a proposal, sending it to publishers, writing the book, and correcting the proofs. I took two positive uphill steps when I wrote the proposal and sent it off. Of course, it may be a false summit. I could not get a positive reply, so I had to take a different route to my destination.

- **It changes the world:** Creativity is needed when something new is required. The very term "innovation" incorporates the Latin word for new. If an existing solution, an existing product, or an existing approach did, there would be no need for creativity. We could carry on the way we always had. In simple terms, creativity positively plunges us into the reservoir of ideas rather than misdirection and hoping something will float out.

Fostering Creativity in Your Business

Cultures don't exist in theory—they exist only in practice. So this section deals with the heart of the subject, and, unsurprisingly, there is much to say! We will examine the critical motivators that act as incentives for fostering creativity in your business.

It would make life easy if the difference between innovative and conventional organizations could be boiled down to one or two critical factors: "Innovative organizations do X and Y, and conventional organizations don't. So, to become an innovative organization, you must fix X and Y, and everything will be fine." Unfortunately, life is more complex than that; the difference between the two types of organization isn't just a few characteristics but a few involved steps:

- **Set the stage for brainstorming:** As the owner and CEO of your business, you have an enormously important role in determining whether or not an organization is genuinely innovative, mainly because you can make things happen or block things you don't like. An organization that allows its employees to contribute to the business and grooms and promotes those passionate about its success already creates the stage for innovation to thrive.

- **Encourage individuality:** Innovation, at any point, is rarely a solitary activity, so rewarding only one person will put other contributors at a disadvantage. However, the issue here is to strike a balance between, on the one hand, being seen to encourage innovation and also offering a reward to a deserving individual and, on the other, being seen to be fair. My experience is that public awards to individuals should be modest in value but high in prestige (more value can permanently be assigned to the annual bonus) to avoid jealousy and accusations of unfairness; public awards to small teams are, in my view, better. But even with a team award, there will always be someone on the outside.

- **Provide a stimulating atmosphere:** To make innovation happen within your business, some things will have to change: the reward system, how budgets are allocated, possibly the criteria for promotion, or perhaps the overall attitude to risk. Whatever it is that needs to be changed, introducing the change, pushing it through, and making it stick all demand every ounce of all the familiar characteristics of providing a stimulating environment—that is, being able to visualize how much better the future will be when you move from “here” to “there,” building the correct political consensus and keeping things going when they get tough. This is all hard work, and we all have a day job. So don't embark on this course of action if you don't have the will to see it through. It is far better not to start than to start and give up.

- **Embed innovation in everyday practices:** The ultimate objective of creating a genuinely unlearning organization is to make creativity and innovation a natural feature of daily existence, a regular aspect of "the way we do things around here." Innovation isn't something "special," something we go away to do at off-site meetings, or the unique preserve of that department—where is it now?—oh yes, somewhere in marketing, I think. Wise entrepreneurs should embed innovation in their day job and incorporate the tools, techniques, and processes in their daily tasks. The easiest way to embed innovation in your day job is to start facilitating anonymous suggestions at meetings and conversations and act on the good ideas provided.

Overall, innovation and creativity are skills that can be learned. Still, since the conventional educational systems do not teach them, it is up to organizations to correct this in their internal training activities. Innovation and creativity are, therefore, essential components of a wise organization's training and development programs. Once innovation is a natural part of the "way we do things around here," this program will likely comprise a series of "masterclasses" to keep people refreshed and some induction training for new joiners. Still, for organizations seeking to move from "here" to "there," a backlog of skill enhancement needs to be addressed using a unique training initiative.

Action Points

Here are some fun activities for you to do to find the spark and see how you can teach creativity and innovation in your business:

1. Do you encourage creativity in your business?

____

____

____

2. If your answer to the previous question is no, list how to foster creativity in your business and get great ideas from your employees.

____

____

____

3. From this vast number of ideas of all different shapes and sizes you have garnered, perhaps during meetings and conversations, try to distinguish the "good" from the "bad" to simplify the implementation process.

___

___

___

4. It would help if you worked on creating training programs, such as masterclasses, on teaching your employees the concept of creativity and what they stand to gain.

___

___

___

"Without data, you're just another person with an opinion."- W. Edwards Deming

---

CHAPTER ELEVEN

Know Your Tribe

Although markets have significantly changed nowadays, the fundamentals remain unaltered. A call is still nothing more or less than an opportunity to buy or sell. The significant difference lies in locating the market, supplying it with commodities, and securing payment. Calls have ceased as local assemblies or fairs at some crossroads or other central locations. A modem market is limited in scope by the number of possible product users worldwide. The introduction of money, transportation improvements, manufacturing, and many other factors have specialized and complicated the original simplicity of markets.

Markets are measurable; they do not just happen. They follow and are governed by specific economic laws. We cannot solve marketing problems more accurately and readily. It is not due to any irregularity like the markets themselves but rather to our ignorance of the facts that bear upon the situation. If we owned all the data, it is safe to say that markets would be as measurable, specific, and determinable as any other phenomenon that obeys fixed laws. Markets are real, tangible, definite things. They may be plotted, charted, mapped, and reckoned with just as accurately as our knowledge of the facts will allow. And this is where market analysis is needed.

Analyzing the market makes it possible for entrepreneurs to apply proven methods and principles to problems connected with the nature, extent, and peculiarities of the market, together with the means for bringing the product to the market and distributing it there. Just as every branch of science is built upon facts, conducting market analysis helps reveal all possible pertinent facts.

What Is the Goal of Market Analysis?

The market analysis aims to provide insight into the northwest corridor's existing transportation system and travel market. This analysis seeks to evaluate needs and facilities, identify mobility problems, assess the extent of the issues affecting the business, and lay the groundwork for conceptual alternatives to address the corridor's business problems. Some of the benefits of market analysis include the following:

- **Identifying potential customers:** One of the most overlooked methods of getting new customers is to understand current customers, and the only possible way to do so is by conducting a market analysis. It will let you know when they buy from you, what they purchase, etc. For instance, if you own a clothing store, you want to know if your customers purchase protection from the elements, style, image, and prestige. If you don't know your customers, you will waste time and money offering the wrong benefits to bad people. Remember, people don't buy your product or service for what it is; they buy it for what it does precisely for them.

- **Knowing competitors:** Many successful businesses realize that the more they understand their competitors, the easier it is to get customers. Let's face it—your competition wants your customers, and you want theirs. When you conduct a market analysis, you can tell who these competitors are. Due to specialization, you may have only four or five major competitors in your area. You can consider starting a file on each one. It should contain their print and Yellow Pages ads, brochures, coupons, etc.

- **Finding your competitors' strengths and weaknesses:** The data from market analysis gives you the power to understand everything your firm can provide your future customers that your competition cannot. Determine the needs of your current and prospective customers, which your competitors have overlooked. You will think about how your firm can customize an existing product or service or even add a new one that could help you find new customers.

- **Planning for success:** The old maxim, "If you fail to plan, you have planned to fail," is accurate, so you must do market analysis. You want your plan to be a usable living blueprint, not a document in your bookcase collecting dust.

Market Analysis Methods

Many decision-makers (especially entrepreneurs) not only have to understand the goal of market analysis, but they also have to be familiar with methods that can qualify and quantify markets. Although many activities fall under the broad umbrella of market analysis, we want to focus on techniques used to determine potentials and identify and assess likely needs.

- **Interviews:** Interviewing has clear advantages over other methods of obtaining information. If, for instance, the investigation were on the market for a food product in a particular city, it would be far better to interview all the principal dealers in that city than to send them questionnaires. It is certain that, even at best, only a tiny percentage would answer the questionnaire, whereas a majority would register their opinions when questioned in person. If, on the other hand, the investigation were national in scope, then a written questionnaire would have to be used, or perhaps a combination of both, by using the interview in certain selected sections and using questionnaires for the rest of the country. An adequately qualified interviewer can get much information the questionnaire cannot provide. He can obtain opinions, theories, and suggestions. He will hear comments on competing products. The degree of accuracy in results is probably more significant, provided the interview is satisfactory. Fuller results will be of no particular value in a tabular questionnaire.

- **Focus groups:** Typical focus groups you are already familiar with are our trade association reports and booklets, trade magazines, SBA publications, the Small Business Reporter (Bank of America), and newsletters. You should review and recontact these sources if you feel they can assist you in answering any of the questions on your master list.

- **Product/service use research:** The product or service is vital to the success of most retail businesses, whether they are restaurants, convenience food stores, dry cleaning shops, antique shops, etc.

- **Observation-based research:** Observation-based research is the primary market research tool of consumer product companies. If your business opportunity involves manufacturing and marketing a consumer product, you should probably understand the more detailed consumer market research approaches.

- **Market segmentation research:** A widely used technique for analyzing markets is separating the total market for a product or service into segments composed of those customers with similar characteristics. Marketing strategies are then developed to reach those segments of interest to the firm. The basic steps that should be performed when segmenting markets involve identifying the purpose of segmentation, defining terms, establishing limits, establishing requirements for segments, determining bases for segmentation—such as consumer products/services and industrial products/services—collecting data; analyzing details, and, finally, formulating strategies. Naturally, not everyone using this book will agree that these topics are worth pursuing. Thus, I recommend you search for readers dedicated to this subject.

Other market analysis approaches include pricing, competitor analysis, customer satisfaction and loyalty, brand awareness, and campaign research. There is little left to do but decide to start at this point in the analysis process.

Conducting Market Analysis Like a Pro

Here are the steps you need to follow to conduct market analysis like a pro:

- **Determine the purpose of your study:** Conducting market analysis should begin with the question: why is this analysis being performed? The purpose of the market analysis must be clear to the person acting the activity and (if they are different parties) to the person making decisions based on the resulting data. Reasons for conducting market research could be to assess business threats, overcome marketing obstacles, create opportunities, enter new markets, etc. For example, suppose you want to expand into a very different market (like a soft drink firm contemplating entering the citrus drink market). In that case, you need to analyze the market to learn more about the customers of this new market. Or you may wish to use market analysis to reassess your present market and marketing mix (like a health club that wants to identify the types of people interested in its health facilities to better focus its promotional efforts and in-house services).

- **Look at your industry's outlook:** In your analysis, you want to define specific parameters such as market size, current trends, plan, etc. Such definitions flow from the objectives established in Step 1. A proper balance is needed when looking at your industry's outlook.

- **Pinpoint target customers:** For instance, if your market is narrowly defined, the results may be too specific to be of marketing value. Conversely, if your need is defined too broadly, the results will likely be of little practical value from a marketing perspective. Thus, it is essential to identify who should be included as market members. Should it have only the actual users of the product or services, or should it also include persons who influence the purchase? Should it include only present customers or anyone who has purchased the product or service? Should it include individuals or broader purchasing units such as households, institutions, production departments, and buying agents? You want to consider geographic limits too. Should the market contain all the people or firms who might use the product or only those within the geographic boundaries presently served by the firm? Establishing such limitations determines the market size and affects the resulting segments because regional differences may influence how the product is used.

– **Gather extra data:** Your greatest market analysis asset is getting unbiased, relevant, and honest data. The more information you have, the better your business decisions will be. For instance, if users' characteristics are the basis for segmentation, then definitions of different categories of users should be established. For example, if product usage is the basis, the following categories might result: heavy user—uses the product at least twice a month; light user—uses product less than twice a month; nonuser—has not used the product in the last six months. If customer loyalty is the primary basis, then relevant terms need to be defined: loyal customer—purchases product X at least 60% of the time this product category is purchased. You want to make sure you use and rely on credible sources when putting together additional data. Some seeds you can use include The Bureau of Labor Statistics, Trade journal articles, Target market surveys or questionnaires, competitors' strengths and weaknesses, and some of the methods discussed in the previous section.

- **Analyze your findings:** Another critical question when conducting market analysis is: "How will the findings be used?" Whether the study provides insight into a new market or enhances a firm's knowledge of its existing market(s), it is critical to specify how the results will be incorporated into its marketing efforts. Stating the purpose of the analysis at the outset establishes the amount of effort and expenditures needed in the remaining steps of the process. Earlier in the previous soft drink example, the firm planned to use the analysis to disclose how and where citrus drinks are consumed—information that would help them evaluate various distribution channels. The health club example involved a firm that planned on using the analysis results to uncover niches in the exercise market they might pursue (special classes for older people or workout facilities for people with disabilities).

- **Put your analysis into action:** While it could be tedious to conduct a market analysis, your business can only benefit from it when you put all your discoveries into action. Once the necessary data or information has been identified, you want to develop a marketing strategy using the four P's of marketing—price, product, place, and promotion—to satisfy the needs of the segments' members. Meanwhile, don't just pack up all your analysis and dump it somewhere; revisit your market analysis frequently and make modifications to suit your current marketing goals. You can also consult more books and resources to learn how to develop strategies to conduct "high potential" market analysis.

Although every market investigation's fundamental principles are the same, the individual problem demands individual treatment. Ordinarily, this requires a man with the proper training and habits and a thorough grasp of business principles. The success of a market analysis depends on both the man and the method, each supplementing the other. The man supplies, by judgment and experience, sufficient and satisfying data. The technique puts the procedure's steps in order and collates them.

Action Points

1. Outline how you can apply market analysis to your business.

____

____

____

2. What specific results are you looking to achieve with market analysis?

____

____

____

3. Which market analysis tool would you like to use for your business?

____

____

____

"When money realizes it is in good hands, it wants to stay and multiply in those hands." – Idowu Koyenikan

CHAPTER TWELVE

Smart Money Entrepreneur

I If you've run a business before, managed budgets at a previous job, or are good at handling your own money, you might find it easy to track your business's finances and keep the books in order. But if this is all new to you, and you are particularly math-phobic, you might worry that tracking and managing your business's income and expenses are dreadfully tricky tasks. Thankfully, this is an overblown (but widespread) fear. Managing business finances can be pretty straightforward, even for people who aren't true “money.”

As with many aspects of running a business, the trick is establishing a system early on to help you stay organized. With a plan in place—and by “system,” I mean a simple process for managing your receipts and files as well as having money management principles to abide by—you'll be able to handle most or all of your financial tasks, even if you've never done it before. While experience with managing money certainly won't hurt, the basics are not hard to master, even for the inexperienced.

Don't be afraid if you're keen on launching your business but still worried there's so much to learn quickly. You don't have to turn into a financial guru overnight. In practice, I advise every small business owner to consult at least once or twice during their start-up days with an experienced finance officer (or possibly two) to help them start on the right track. In addition, consulting an expert will help you overcome obstacles in your financial learning curve, especially if you're a novice.

This chapter overviews what's involved in essential money management for small businesses. We will cover money-related concepts and practical tasks entrepreneurs must understand, including making a budget, taking inventory, and minimizing expenses.

Separate Business and Personal Finances

Over time, I have met far too many new business owners and entrepreneurs who sheepishly admit they do not have a separate business bank account and have been running their whole operation with their bank account. These people mix business and personal finances. This is a huge financial mistake for several reasons. One is that if you hope to protect your assets by creating an LLC or a corporation, you'll throw any such protection out the window by mixing your personal and business funds. Other reasons for not mixing your finances with your business may include tax, professional image, ability to leverage, business credit application, etc. Here's how to separate your business money from your money:

- **Separate receipts:** The process starts with keeping actual receipts, usually of all the expenses made and all the income earned. This means carefully keeping and organizing your expense records (such as bills from the office supply store, invoices for your web hosting charges, and receipts of payments to your employees and freelancers) and your income receipts (such as a cash register tape of your cafe's income, check stubs from your client's payment checks, or your invoices to clients marked "Paid").

- **Obtain an EIN:** You should use your Social Security number if you run your business alone with no employees. However, you must obtain an Employer Identification Number if you have employees or are a corporation or partnership. You can do so by applying for it, and in about three weeks, you will get your number, which you will need to open bank accounts for the business.

- **Incorporate your business:** Registering your business may seem like a job for a lawyer. After all, it would help if you studied a lot of paperwork and complex corporate and tax laws. There is paperwork, and some work is needed, but you can do it yourself. Setting up a company is a relatively simple and easy process. It all starts with choosing a corporate name, preparing and filing articles of incorporation, setting up a corporate records book, preparing your bylaws, appointing initial corporate directors, preparing minutes of the first board meeting, and issuing shares of stock. It would help if you did more activities after you formed your corporation, and you can learn about them from different online sources.

- **Open a business bank account:** On a more critical day-to-day level, mixing your business transactions with personal transactions will make it impossible to do the simple financial management tasks described in this chapter. So you should run (do not walk) to your local community bank and open a business bank account as soon as you launch.

- **Apply for business credit:** Businesses rely upon recognition to expand their markets and find customers. More people can buy if they provide credit purchase options for their customers. Many customers lack the funds to pay cash or prefer to use credit to purchase and pay later. A business soon realizes that many competitors offer credit plans. A company will need to accept the use of credit if it wants to survive.

- **Pay yourself a salary:** Another way to create a formal boundary between your personal and business accounts is by paying yourself a salary. Also, if your S corporation or LLC makes a profit, pay yourself a reasonable wage. You can almost guarantee an audit if you submit a return without reported compensation.

Always Have a Budget

Budgeting is more than just the job we have to do to meet the needs of our finance department. Budgeting can help your team succeed, but sometimes, it can help you find mistakes. It's much better to spot errors in your budget plan than have problems with your business later because you didn't notice them. Good planning usually reduces project costs by about a tenth. But before explaining how to create a simple budget for your business, consider a reasonable budget.

Time is a significant factor in budgeting. Are you planning a budget for days, weeks, months, or years? Budgeting for days and weeks can be helpful at home, but business is mainly run for months and years. So, let's start with this. Budgets for one year or less are usually called short-term budgets, and budgets for one year or more are called long-term budgets. One of the reasons to think over the years is that many things tend to repeat themselves in the yearly cycle. Secondly, companies file tax returns yearly, so it's a good idea to track what we do depending on the fiscal year. Besides, the best budgets are usually simple and flexible. It usually includes specific components such as your estimated revenue, fixed costs, variable costs, one-off costs, cash flow, profit made, and a budget calculator.

Meanwhile, you must think about the quirks of your industry and the type of business you do before you create a budget for your business. The reason is that the budget framework of business differs. Now, let's proceed to the steps you need to follow to create a budget for your business.

- **Estimate monthly fixed costs:** These costs come from one of two sources. These can be known costs based on mortgages, service contracts, or equipment leases. Another possibility is that prices fluctuate but do not increase or decrease; they fluctuate monthly and, on average, over a year or two.

- **Determine variable expenses:** These are expenses that change from month to month. So, you need to show costs that you think will vary month by month, or you may estimate payments based on a project plan.

- **Predict one-time costs:** A good example is a project expected to take three years at $5,000 per year. It's happening from 2021-2025, so the first year shows up in your five-year budget, but the second to fifth do not show up until the next budget plan.

- **Project revenues:** Unless you have a working crystal ball, the best way to predict revenues is to picture it. Ask people what they want and what is going on, and make rough or calculated guesses. Your guess is the best possible lead based on reliable information, experience, careful thinking, and accurate calculations.

- **Track your profit (or loss):** Another approach is to estimate your income on each product or service you sell. You may find that products and services are sold to different markets or at other times of the year. You should estimate monthly sales for each item and then add them to see the total income (profit and loss) per month and year.

- **Plan regular budget reviews:** It's time to ask yourself some questions before you finish up the budget. Does it make sense? Are the numbers correct for every listed item? Think about your decisions and make sure you are happy with them. If not, ask someone or think for yourself. You'll want to confirm if your numbers add up even using a spreadsheet program or software. You also want to pay more attention to the items with higher figures.

- **Make adjustments:** You are almost ready to present your budget. But you are probably a bit nervous—and you should be! You don't want someone else to find your mistakes after you've delivered your budget. So, the best thing is to find those mistakes or help someone else. And it never hurts to take a few extra minutes to make adjustments; these include making the document look good with stylish, professional fonts and formatting.

Having a budget for your business will also help cut down unnecessary expenses. Total operating income and total operating expenses should generally match. If your organization's expense goals exceed income goals, meaning that anticipated costs will exceed anticipated income, then you have to make a plan to increase revenue and reduce projected expenses. Be prepared to take corrective measures later (such as cutting budgeted costs or generating additional income). Track expenses diligently. Formally decide to use the organization's unrestricted funds to make a difference.

Take Inventory

The most crucial aspect of understanding inventory is to realize that it may be a significant financial investment for the company, often the only major capital investment needed to operate the business. In recent times, and in the potential future, two powerful economic forces have exerted strong and consistent pressure on this investment for virtually every inventory-intensive business. They are:

- The continually rising cost of acquiring the inventory is driven by various inflationary forces, such as transportation costs, energy costs, and a relative scarcity of raw materials, to name a few.
- The increasing cost of capital, both debt financing and equity. Awareness of the impact of capital decisions is usually limited to top management but is present, nonetheless.

Smaller firms must grow solely through retained earnings since obtaining public equity capital sources is far more difficult now than before. As interest rates hover in the range of 15–20%, it becomes increasingly difficult to justify either investing the company's cash assets in inventory when higher returns are often available elsewhere at lower risk or continuing in business at a lower rate of return.

From an accounting point of view, inventory is items purchased as part of the cost of goods sold. It is a business expense. If each purchased item were sold the day it was received, no capital investment would be required for inventory, regardless of the volume of business.

Without similar grouping items, an inventory manager would be forced to manage each item individually. Assigning codes of various types to each part number allows us to use the information pyramid concept to manage inventory investment. Rather than assign codes randomly, one must consider the purpose and the task to be facilitated by the code. These tasks can be grouped into five major areas: control codes, purchase codes, scheduling and stocking orders, cost codes, and special codes. However, not all will necessarily occur in every business. A given area may use more than one code to accomplish its purposes.

Action Points

1. Do you manage your personal and business finances together or separately?

____

____

____

2. Do you have a budget for your business?

____

____

____

3. How often do you take inventory?

4. Write out ways you can follow to reduce the expenses you make in your business.

5. Outline what you need to improve your money management skills.

"We don't have to be smarter than the rest. We have to be more disciplined than the rest."— Warren Buffett

CHAPTER THIRTEEN

Investing in a Small Business

Starting and running a business involves a mountain of work, especially if you want to do it right. However, suppose you structure things by investing in someone else's business. In that case, you can avoid the hassle of day-to-day operations and still participate in the growth of a profitable business. So, if you have a knack for identifying small companies with potential, you might be able to make rewarding investments that aren't too taxing.

Investing in preexisting SMEs can be risky but rewarding. The best option is the one you are familiar with—either equity or debt investments. If you learn about a new business idea from someone you know and trust, try to do minor research and make the best decisions. A company or idea can be an excellent investment. We aim to highlight ways to invest in a small business and do it with your first profits.

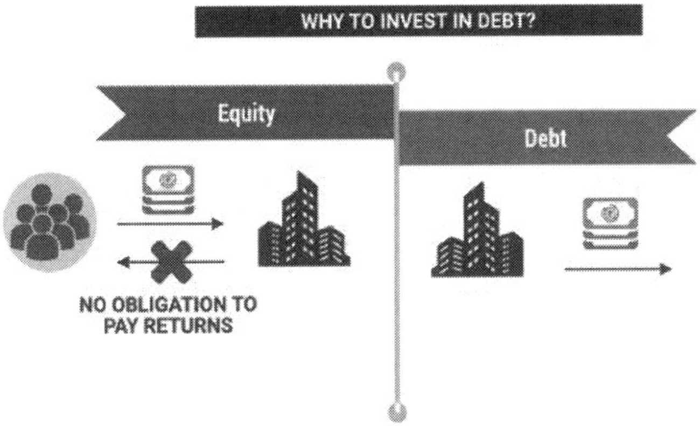

How to Invest in Small Businesses

Of course, it's not only individuals who need money; businesses are looking for money too. To continue operating and be successful, every business needs to have cash readily available for such things as meeting its payroll, stocking inventory, and buying supplies and parts. Previously, companies usually had a line of credit or would go to their bank and borrow money. Today, however, things have changed. Small businesses can now seek funding through various means, all of which fall back on the two foundations we will discuss.

Equity investing

An equity investment is an investment in a private company in exchange for a share of ownership. In a broad sense, equity investments are securities of a private company representing that company or potential property. Investors must invest in private equity using debt financing or direct investment.

Understanding the complexity of private equity is essential for communicating intelligently and competently with business angels. Quite frankly, this is important if you want to avoid serious problems.

Equity investments come in all shapes and sizes. These include preferred shares (where you have preemptive rights, priorities, and privileges) and common stock (where you are on the same level as the company's founder).

Equity investments have regional and regional trends, terminology, specifics, and regulatory requirements that must work with people to help companies recognize and work within these parameters. Therefore, before investing in a company, you need to secure advisers (including legal counsel) who are experienced in and knowledgeable about equity investing on a local and national level.

Debt investing

Making a debt investment in a small business means you loan your money to the company. In return, you receive a promise to pay back your money with interest at some point in the future. You have many choices for your debt investments, including certificates of deposit at banks and savings institutions, debt capital, municipal bonds, corporate bonds, annuities, some insurance policies, loans to friends, and mortgages.

Let's examine this example to understand the relationship between bond prices and interest rates. If you buy a $10,000 bond, paying $1,000 interest yearly, you earn 10%. If the market interest rates rise to 12%, you still earn $1,000 annually (10% of your investment). If you want to sell your bond, the buyer would expect to make 12% of his investment. To do this, he will not be willing to pay you the entire $10,000. Conversely, if market interest rates decrease to 8% when you want to sell, your buyer would expect to pay more than $10,000 to receive $ 1,000 per year in interest.

Inflation might rob you of your buying power, assuming your debt investment is held to maturity and you receive all your money back. If inflation is higher than your after-tax rate of return, you can buy fewer groceries with your investment after the term compared to when you invested.

Other risks you face with debt investments are the failure of the borrower to repay the debt, loss of value of the investment due to future interest rate changes, and the loss of buying power due to inflation. It would help to consider these genuine risks before making your investment decisions.

Despite these risks, there are good reasons to use this investment. The most important reason is that you need a regular cash income, monthly or quarterly. These debt investments will usually give you the most reliable source of cash flow. Another important reason for using debt as part of your portfolio is diversification. Diversification is one of the best ways to reduce overall risk in your investment portfolio. If you have a specific need within a few years, these investments may be a secure way to store your funds until they are needed.

You have many debt investments to choose from. The easiest to understand is a certificate of deposit issued by a bank or other financial institution. It is very similar to a savings account. The significant difference is that you have committed your money to stay in your account for a specified period before you remove it. If you withdraw your funds before the expiration of that time limit, you will be penalized for early withdrawal. The institution will pay you a higher interest rate than on a savings account in exchange for your promise to lock away your money for some time. Typically, the longer the term of the deposit, the higher the interest rate. The time can range anywhere from one month to several years.

Equity investments vs. debt investments

There are two ways to invest in a small business: loans (debt financing) or investments (equity financing). When you invest in a company under the terms of a loan agreement (sometimes called the "note"), the business owner must repay the loan with interest. If you invest in an enterprise, on the other hand, you get partial ownership, usually in the form of stock in your corporation. So, for a business to explore equity financing, it must have a business entity that can accommodate investment—generally, a limited liability company or corporation.

The advantage of a loan is that it is not an investment. In other words, the business owner is not giving up any ownership in their enterprise, and the lender has no management say or direct entitlement to profits in your business. The business owner's obligation to the lender is to repay the loan on time, and the interest payments can be deducted at tax time.

The disadvantage of a loan is the debt—the looming monthly payments and the risk of personal liability (if the loan is guaranteed), loss of property (if the loan is secured), or a lawsuit if there is a default on the loan payments. In a worst-case scenario—in which you secured the loan or guaranteed it—defaulting could result in the loss of business, attachment of wages, or a judgment that could be used against the business owner's property.

The advantages of equity investments are that business owners don't have to repay investors if their business goes under, and their personal property won't likely be at risk. Business owners may also get advice and guidance from those vested in your business's success.

The disadvantage of equity investments is that you get a more significant piece of the pie because you own a share of the business. And if you, as the investor, may seek to control the company or offer help.

The problem of the preferred equity-debt hybrid

Sometimes, you might be torn between equity and debt investments. But based on all this information about debt and equity investing, I would always recommend you weigh their pros and cons before deciding on your investment course. Also, it would help if you considered your level of comfort. The risks of debt or equity and your investing philosophies.

Ways You Can Invest Your Company's Profits

As your business grows, you will make more money and might begin to wonder what you could do with them. To maintain a competitive edge and offer the quality of service that clients demand, it's better to invest and reinvest your company's profit. Reinvesting in your business is one key strategy for growth. Just as you need capital to get things off the ground, you need more money to expand your enterprise. And to help out with the process, I have put together some of the best ways you can do so:

- **Business improvement:** You can choose to use the company's profit to make improvements in your business, such as getting new infrastructure and better equipment, creating website and SEO improvements, increasing your marketing and advertising presence, or researching different ways to grow the business. Apple started by making computers, but the company didn't settle for that; instead, it dug deeper and found a new market in iPods. If, for instance, you've started with essential equipment (one com-puter and a printer), you'll need to keep reinvesting some of your income to expand and provide extra services. A painless way to save for these items without going further into debt is to take 5% or 10% of every check you receive and put it aside for future investment. This method has allowed my office to go from essential equipment (one computer and printer) to three separate systems, three printers, a fax machine, a scanner, graphics boards, additional fonts and programs, a copier, and many other items.

- **Hire help:** Even if you attract new customers, can you do all the work? Hiring employees is one solution, but they may need time to be trained in how you operate. If you've got too much going on, quality might suffer, which won't please any of your old or new customers. So, hire new employees and try to outsource your least favorite tasks.

- **Don't diversify too early:** Remember that trying to grow too quickly has sunk many businesses. Reinvesting profits is a tried-and-true approach for building a business's overall worth, but this often means there's no cash available for emergencies or slow periods. There's also the problem of simply taking on too much. So, you want to take your time to see if your business has grown to that stage where it needs diversification.

Overall, before investing in a project, ask to see a copy of the business plan and ensure everything needed for the successful running of the business has been put in place. Thoroughly check out the people running the business. Talk to others who don't have a stake in the idea and learn from their comments and concerns. But don't forget that many intelligent people have rained on the parade of what turned out to be a terrific business idea.

Action Points

1. What are your investment goals? Write them out in your book.

____
____
____

2. List small businesses you would like to invest in.

____
____
____

3. Which investing method is your preferred option—equity or debt investments?

____
____
____

4. Write how you intend to spend or invest your company's profits.

____
____
____

"Time is the scarcest resource; unless it is managed, nothing else can be managed." - Peter Drucker

---

CHAPTER FOURTEEN

Business Management Tools

Technology is the most important story in business today and is straightforward. This is because recent advances in digital technology have lifted restrictions and created new, exciting opportunities that affect everyone's life and business. Want to finally listen to your customers and escape the narrow lenses of research and focus groups? Social media allows you. Do you want to be accessible and productive for everyone, wherever you are? Mobile computing makes this possible. Do you want to make more accurate predictions and decisions in critical areas? This is the promise of big data. Are you looking to deploy entirely new organizational structures, business processes, and products to customers and quickly change them over time as circumstances change? We've all seen companies do it all, so we all know it's possible.

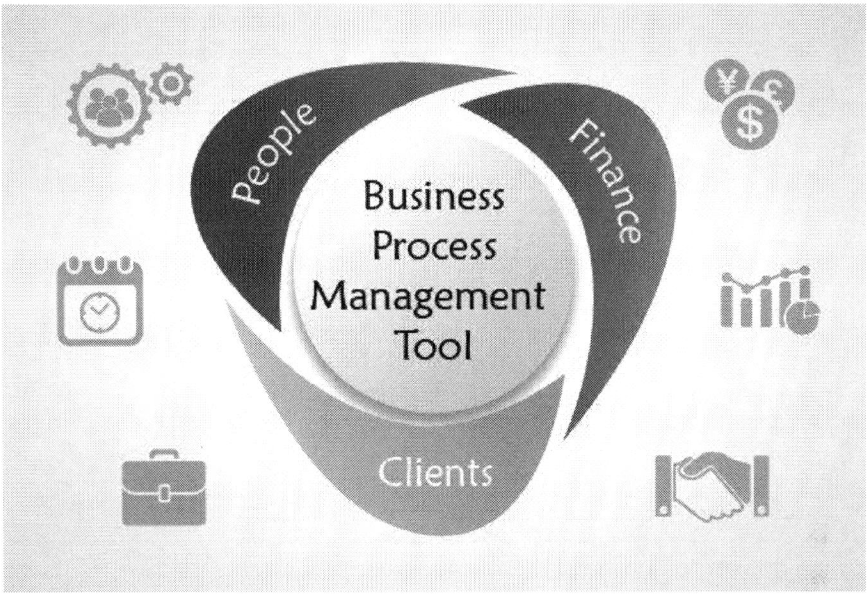

I have found that owning and running a small business can be fun and rewarding at the same time. This is not always the case. And when something hits the fan, the fun idea is to go first. However, learning to organize and keep track of things can be exciting and rewarding.

Because I run my own business, I've had the chance to use different excellent business tools and software. I have seen many appealing programs that have helped automate my business, increase productivity, and make more money with less trouble. And just like me, if you're serious, you may have even gone to a computer show or your local computer store and been impressed by what the equipment can do. Today, with the help of technology in my business, it is possible to do good work, succeed, and enjoy the process.

Therefore, to see your business move to the next level of growth and success, you must work on automating some routine tasks so you can focus on other vital areas of your business. And that is precisely what business management tools allow us to do. So, our focus in this chapter is to explore some of these tools and software.

Project Task Management Tools

A project is any highly complex task that involves many subtasks, detailed scheduling, and complicated monitoring techniques. It can range from conducting a study, producing a film, planning the annual sales conference, or masterminding a corporate acquisition. Although many more straightforward projects and tasks can be handled manually by making a master list, working on too many jobs can be complicated.

Fortunately, project management tools such as Trello, Asana, Kissflow, etc., are a priceless addition to any business that desires to synchronize projects between the team members, save valuable time, stick to their schedule, and meet their goals more efficiently. These project management tools allow you to set goals and deadlines, break a project into subtasks, and group related subtasks into working blocks. You can also organize subtasks into an appropriate progression (either a sequential line of development or a parallel line of product), delegate specific tasks or tasks to subordinates and outside consultants, and monitor fewer complex tasks with calendar tickler files and referral folders.

Marketing Automation

Marketing is all about getting more customers and making sales. The more you know about your present and future customers and the more you will use your knowledge to serve them better, the more customers you will retain, and the more successful your enterprise will become. In today's highly competitive marketplace, success depends on how well you market your business and keep up with changing customer needs. The rule is simple: focus on your customers' needs and make sure they are satisfied in some way by what you provide.

Using marketing tools and software in your business will help increase the value of your enterprise and your work. These tools include AWeber, GetResponse, Leadpages for email marketing, Facebook Business for Facebook and Instagram advertising, ClickMagick for tracking and analysis, SEO plugins, and more.

Enterprise Resource Planning (ERP)

Enterprise resource planning (ERP) systems are an enterprise marvel that impacts the business and information technology worlds. Enterprise resource planning systems such as SAP, Oracle, NetSuite, and Sage provide enterprises with a transaction processing model that integrates with other enterprise activities such as production planning and human resources. Implement a standard corporate process and a unified database covering a range of corporate activities and locations. ERP systems provide integration across multiple sites and functional areas.

As a result, the ERP system has improved the decision-making function, manifesting itself in many indicators, such as inventory reduction (raw materials, work in progress, finished goods), staff reduction, and acceleration of settlement processing. Thus, you can use ERP to help businesses create value. In fact, ERP contributes to creating value by changing the essential nature of an organization in various ways.

Customer Relationship Management

Customer relationship management (CRM) means different things to different people. Even the meaning of the three-letter abbreviation CRM is disputed. Most people use CRM to view customer relationship management. Others use CRM to refer to customer relationship marketing. Another group prefers "customer management," dropping the term "relationship," assuming that not all customers want a relationship with a supplier. Still, others choose self-expression marketing. Be that as it may, CRM is a customer-centric business practice. For our research, we refer to CRM as a software application that automates a company's marketing, sales, and service functions.

Top CRM platforms like Zoho CRM, Pipedrive CRM, and Oracle Sales Cloud focus on developing a customer-centric business culture. This culture aims to attract and retain customers by creating and delivering more value than our competitors. Culture is reflected in management behavior, the structure of the company's formal system, and myths and stories created within the company. In a customer-centric culture, resources are allocated to maximize customer value, employee behaviors that increase customer satisfaction are rewarded, and customer information is collected, shared, and applied across the business.

Finance and Accounting

The variety of personal finance software products available today results from evolutionary advancements that have come of age. Although initially designed for home use, these packages are now popular as tools for small businesses. The software can provide nearly all the accounting help you need to run your small business. While it can't replace your accountant, it can make cash-flow management more leisurely and less expensive.

When choosing a finance and accounting program, identify the features you want or need. Aside from features, ease of use and cost are two major factors. Please don't buy the more sophisticated package you need; it will add to the price and might be more complicated to use. Under tax laws, most software packages require the single-entry bookkeeping system for sole proprietorships and closely-held partnerships. Double-entry accounting can be complex and costly for many small business entrepreneurs. Some of the best finance and accounting software available today include QuickBooks, Xero, FreshBooks, Wave, etc.

Inventory Management Tools

Inventory management is a topic that has some degree of relevance for almost every organization. While inventory investment ties up money that could be invested in other areas, it generates a payback when adequately managed. However, the type of items in an organization's inventory will vary considerably. In all organizations, management has a common interest in a more effective inventory management process, which can mean inventory cost reductions, inventory performance improvements, or both. The best business inventory tools you can use include Orderhive, inFlow, Zoho Inventory, etc. You will manage your small businesses' inventory effectively with the right tools.

Social Media Management

Companies have instituted social media technology in experimental and business transformation phases. The testing phase was all about the tools. Companies leveraged social media components, such as blogs, product ratings, discussion forums, and customer comments, as one-offs—isolated and often uncoordinated initiatives that paid little attention to the existing technical infrastructure. These tools were usually tied to a specific campaign meant to have a short-term impact, for example, giving the chief executive officer a voice to comment on a pressing public issue or giving customers a chance to weigh in on a new product concept. But we are past the experimental stage. Today, social media platforms are used in a larger, more strategic context—they are how companies manage their entire customer relationships. Creating great Web experiences for customers is a crucial goal of customer relationship management (CRM) technologies today, and social media has become a vital part of those Web experiences. Luckily, we have hundreds of social media tools that help to fulfill this purpose. These include Hootsuite and Buffer (platforms for managing multiple social media platforms), Sprout Social (which helps with social media scheduling, monitoring, and reporting), CoSchedule (a marketing calendar for social media), Friends+Me (which allows you to share content anywhere), and lots more.

Human Resource Management

HRM tools make the process of hiring, training, appraising, and compensating employees super easy. Consider what you need to operate a five-person retail store. First, hiring employees might take a list of ads that need help, a job application, an interview checklist, various verifications such as education and immigration status, and a telephone inquiry checklist. Then, you may need employment contracts, nondisclosure and non-competitive contracts, and employer compensation contracts.

You may need a background check, new employee checklist, tax withholding form, and new employee details to process a new employee. Plus, you have to get to work and request personnel data, daily and weekly work time records, employee hourly weekly schedules, and expense reports to track an employee on board. In addition, there are all forms of performance appraisal, disciplinary notices, employee reference documents, employee turnover notices, and recruitment reviews.

The above list only scratches the surface of the policies, procedures, and documents needed to carry out the human resource management portion of the business. Perhaps just one or two employees can keep track of everything in their head or write a separate note for each HR action and place it in each employee's folder. However, as the number of employees increases, you will need a personnel system consisting of standardized forms. Then, as the company expands, you'll automate various parts of the HR system, such as payroll or appraising. Some of the best HR management software include Sapling, Eddy, Sage HRMS, etc.

Perhaps you're already working on a project or know what opportunity or problem you want to start with. If so, dive in and select the appropriate tool or software. If not, take some time to think about which program matters most to your business; several are out there.

Action Points

1. What areas of your business do you think need automation?

____
____
____

2. Which tools and software will best fit your business?

____
____
____

3. Research and write how you intend to use these tools and software to grow your business.

____
____
____

Part III - Building an Empire

"Wealth comes from multiple incomes. Always think of growth and new businesses to create new income streams."— Ehab Atalla

CHAPTER FIFTEEN

Building an Empire

Ever dream of making money through different sources, even while you're still doing your regular job? I'll share the secret behind passive income strategies in this chapter. You've probably heard that the average millionaire has at least seven income streams, which may sound like a straightforward money-making opportunity and something anyone can do. But, you see, all these strategies take work—sometimes lots of work, especially at the beginning of the process. But the concept is to put a system that will generate revenue year after year, almost automatically.

So whether it's just a side hustle you need or a new stream of income, this chapter is for you. It features picking a side hustle or the best possible income stream.

Multiple Income Streams Are the Answer to Your Financial Goals

Building multiple income streams takes plenty of time and effort, but If you master the following live keys, you should make the journey smoother and shorter.

- **Make a list of your skills and passion:** The sweet spot for building a new income stream is to play where talent, skill, and passion meet. Talent is what you're born with. Great comedians have been making people laugh since their earliest school days. But they usually die when they first step up to a mic to perform. This is because pacing, audience interaction, and writing material must still be learned. Passion is another factor you need to consider. Even if you're good at something, you won't excel unless you enjoy it. I am talented and skilled in financial literacy and money management. They're easy for me; I have a lot of practice and am passionate about them, so I have made them a central part of my working life.

- **Be honest about your availability:** Your interests will naturally change, evolve, and expand over time as they do. You can reposition your work to suit. It's possible that what you're currently doing was once exciting and challenging but now feels dull. That's natural. The most exciting projects and tasks are always at the edge of our abilities; once we've mastered them, they lose their shine, and we're ready for the next. We all have different paces at which we like to evolve. What's yours? Are you happy to go deep into a topic and specialize for several years before you move on? Or do you get bored quickly and keep switching to something new to keep your interest? If you're in the latter group that doesn't dedicate enough time to their likes and interests to change frequently, you want something that will retain your interest. They should be multifaceted, have lots of new things to learn, and allow you to use your skills to invent new ideas or do research without having to do all the implementation yourself. You can consider options like comedy, consultations, public speaking, and research, as they allow you to learn quickly, make creative connections, collaborate, and explore.

- **Explore your startup cost and income potential:** You want to estimate how much money you'll need to start your side hustle or new business before starting. Is it an online or remote business that doesn't need an office? How about getting equipment such as a desk, a chair, a phone, computers, and filing cabinets? If, for instance, you want to start up a website design agency, you will need to make a budget for miscellaneous services such as registering your domain name, paying the hosting fees for your website, marketing, etc. And if a business requires a low investment, such as freelancing, you want to look at how much you can expect to make. Your income will vary based on your status; part-time freelancers will have less time to devote to their business and thus take on fewer clients. You can earn about $20,000 in your first year as a freelancer. Your income will increase significantly as you develop your skills and raise your rates.

- **Narrow down your options:** One of the most valuable things you can ever do is learn what you enjoy and don't enjoy doing. It can also be one of the most challenging things to do. Believe it or not, getting to where you want to go can seem straightforward after that! It's Just a list of stuff to do—call someone, write an email, turn up somewhere, and do the work. If you hit an obstacle, someone can tell you how to get around it.

When you know what comes most naturally to you and then center your working life around it, leaving out as much of what you don't like as possible, you will be amazed at how fast your progress can be. Your work will be like play; your passion will attract new opportunities daily, and your competitors will barely concern you.

- **Get started:** Don't wait to be struck by a lightning bolt with insight into what you're meant to be doing with your life. Understand instead that decisions like this are more usually built than happened upon. Build your path to playing brick by brick. Get yourself a notebook to capture your thoughts about your business and goals. Carry it everywhere. Write down everything you discover: what you like and don't like, people whose work or lifestyle you'd like to emulate, ideas for contacts to talk to, projects to try, etc. This is now your playbook. Keep these notes separate from your other thoughts; don't mix them with your diary, creative writing, or laundry list. You must be able to leaf through it quickly and find something you wrote earlier.

Choosing a Passive Income Source

There are many different ways to create passive income streams. One of the most popular ways is to buy real estate, such as apartment units or a store. You've made passive income if you can collect rent that brings in more than you must pay in loan payments and maintenance costs. You must ensure the property remains in good shape, occasionally deal with tenants, address their concerns, write and enforce leases, etc. But, for the most part, the rents will roll in, and—unless a unit remains empty or some unexpected mishap befalls the property—you will keep collecting that income for the foreseeable future.

The strategies I'll share with you are designed to create ongoing income; they will take time, money, and skills to put in place and some ongoing work. But each will continue bringing in steady and automatic income for the long term, with as little effort as possible from you.

- **Affiliate marketing**

If you don't have a product, you can make money by promoting other products and receiving a commission every time someone buys one. Some people make a good living just by doing this. If you're in the habit of recommending other people's good stuff anyway, why not take the commission they're offering? Sounds good, huh? A lot of people seem to think so. As a result, there is a lot of competition out there for affiliate marketers, so just like anything else, you'll need to become good at the skills required—online advertising (to attract website traffic), copywriting (to describe the product), and choosing the right products to offer. But if you like fiddling around on the internet, it can be fun to learn it all, aside from the skills. When you see a product that solves your audience's problems, look for a link to "Our Affiliate Program" or something similar. Often, you can join immediately by filling out a simple form. You can also join affiliate platforms like ClickBank, JVZoo, ShareASale, etc. You will be given a unique link to the product you want to promote. All you have to do is email or write a blog post explaining why you recommend it and include your unique affiliate link. You will automatically earn a commission when someone clicks on it to buy the product.

- **Start a blog**

There are many reasons to get into blogging: it's a way to express your ideas and a great marketing tool. And, yes, it can even earn you money. Very few bloggers make much from their blogs because you need many readers to gain from a blog. Still, it's worth understanding as part of a larger business strategy. Your blog can be monetized through affiliate marketing (as we've just seen), showing adverts (using a service like Google AdWords), promoting and selling your info products, or turning the blog into a membership site where people must pay to subscribe.

- **Education and instructional businesses**

If you have a skill or knowledge in a subject that will help people earn more money, improve their relationships, empower and motivate them to change their lives or learn a skill or craft, people will pay you to teach them. You can teach them privately, in a group, or in workshops or seminars in one- to seven-day sessions. You should have knowledge and firsthand experience in your teaching topic. You should like people, have patience, and break the subject you are teaching into basic steps for learning. You can conduct business, finance, arts, DIY crafts, relationship goals, etc.

- **Antique dealer**

This business requires minimal startup investment. Find antique bargains at thrift shops and yard sale items that cost a fraction of their value; resell them to antique collectors for a significant profit. Every year, items age to antique status. Before you start, study appropriate journals and manuals to know the monetary value of the items you buy. Then, set up booths at fairs, flea markets, and local malls and sell to small antique shops in your area.

- **Auto consultant**

You can quickly run this business from home, requiring little startup investment. Take advantage of your skills in auto repair. Many people are willing to pay for expert advice on choosing a dependable car at a good value. You can become the middleman for buying new or used vehicles from dealerships. Many people don't want to haggle with the salesperson; they don't like to bargain. You can negotiate the sale for them, charging a percentage of everything you save them under the sticker price.

- **Home-based daycare business**

With a home-based daycare, you can provide excellence in child care because you can decide how many full-timers and part-timers you wish to have, and you will not have more than 4–6 children in your respect. You can also specify your preferred age group, creating a relaxing atmosphere for yourself and the children. Before starting this service, check your state's licensing requirements or restrictions.

- **Housekeeping service**

With both parents working in most families today, cleaning services are becoming increasingly popular. Offer various services, including basic cleaning and dusting; offer extras such as cleaning garages, organizing closets, and doing laundry.

Consider getting bonded and insured to encourage customers to trust you more readily.

- **Catering service**

Everyone needs a good caterer at some point for a wedding, an anniversary party, or a romantic dinner for two. Use your unique culinary talents to create beautiful meals that make people want to return for more. You might want to enroll in a culinary school to brush up on your abilities and help you pay close attention to detail. Kick off your business with an open house, inviting local business people and asking them to refer you to their clients. Encourage satisfied clients to tell their friends about you.

- **Home health care**

As the population in America ages, more and more people need medical assistance and help with daily routines. However, many people do not need the extensive nursing home services; these people are turning to home health care for assistance. Keep your business small by providing all the maintenance, or expand your vision and hire other trained individuals to help you.

- **Nutrition expert**

It is well known that most Americans do not always eat healthy foods or adopt beneficial cooking methods. If you see a lot about nutrition, share what you know with others to encourage proper eating and cooking habits. This field is growing, and there is a great need for it. Check out your public library for more information if you want to learn more.

- **Become an expert**

Becoming an expert on your niche topic is vital to succeeding in your online business and making money. However, knowing where to start can be challenging. If you pick a good niche without too much competition and develop the knowledge and skills needed to solve the problems people face, you will find an audience ready for your advice. Use your blog as the central place for people to find you and make the most of social media to reach out and develop your followers. Communicate and share your knowledge and tips via your blog, social media platforms, and, most importantly, by building an email list. You will find that you are building up the numbers on your mailing list to the point where you can start making a good living online. What you are aiming to do is develop preeminence. As Yaro Starak of *Yaro* says, preeminence is essentially a perception. This means that people believe you are the best or at least better than most others at what you do. Because of preeminence, people choose your business over the competition, so you can charge higher prices, and why people seek you out instead of needing to solicit clients.

Always compare the pros and cons of any passive income source and ensure it best fits your skills, interests, and investment goals. Also, you should consider marketing, as some passive income streams need special sales skills to kick off. If you're good at selling, these can be great opportunities. If selling isn't your thing, look for passive income opportunities that need a significant sales effort.

Action Points

1. What steps will you take to build multiple income streams with good cash flow?

____

____

____

2. What skill or set of skills are you looking to hone to build your desired business empire?

____

____

____

3. How do you use your time, skills, or money to increase your income?

____

____

____

4. What three things will you eliminate or reduce to create the time you need to accomplish your goals in a fun and energizing way?

____

____

____

"Returns matter a lot. It's our capital." - Abigail Johnson

CHAPTER SIXTEEN

How to Fund Your Business

Getting the money to fund a business was easier back when there were many options. Banks had ready capital to lend, and loans from agencies like the Small Business Administration (SBA) were available if you did not qualify. If they didn't suit your needs or needed more enormous funding, you could find venture capitalists and angel investors who were more than happy to invest some funds in exchange for a piece of the pie. But those days are long gone due to several factors, such as the housing bubble burst, the mortgage crisis hit, the stock market tumbling, etc. They've all dried up the capital markets.

As a result, today, while many of those funding options are still around, terms and conditions, as they say, apply. There is less money, and it is harder to get. But "harder" is not the same as "impossible." If having less money is the bad news, the good news is that these options are still available, and several new, creative options have also emerged. You need to find the right source to suit your business funding goal. As you already know, it takes money to make money, and new and existing businesses must have access to financial resources to take advantage of good situations. Funds are needed to market new products, pay vendors, meet payrolls, buy equipment, and extend customer credit, to mention a few business activities.

However, money alone will not ensure you a successful operation. Capital, like any resource, must be managed efficiently to maximize profits. While several new small businesses suffer from undercapitalization and funds mismanagement, many cash-rich firms have failed to turn earnings because of poor or inadequate financial management. As a business expands, so do its capital needs. A cash squeeze will occur if growth increases faster than capital availability, causing financial hardship. Likewise, cash flow difficulties will ensue if the business is stagnant due to economic conditions and the availability of capital contracts. We aim to examine the different ways to fund your business idea and understand the factors investors look for before supporting a business.

How to Find Investors for Your Business

In all likelihood, finding the money you need will require that you tap several resources, not just one or two. Let's say that you need $100,000 to start a business. While one loan for the whole amount is possible, what is far more probable is that you might instead use a combination of some of the sources I'll share with you. Financing comes in various forms; if you want to fund your dream, you must be creative and resourceful.

- **Personal savings:** When starting a new business, most people look to their protection and other unique resources as the primary source of capital. Individual resources can mean all sorts of things: savings, money market accounts, stocks and bonds, whole life insurance, and more. Whatever the case, using your assets is usually the first option because it seems complicated to ask anyone to invest in your business—be it a bank, angel investor, uncle, or whoever—if you do not have some of your money supported. Entrepreneurship is a risk. It is a risk of many shades for you: financial, emotional, emotional, and professional. But lenders and investors have little interest in those latter two risks. They want to see that you are willing to accept your fair share of the financial risk, and that is where using your actual capital, like savings, also comes into play. For starters, it proves you are serious.

- **Ask family or friends for capital:** It's safe to say that many, if not most, small businesses begin with at least some funding from friends and family members. It could be a monetary gift or a low-interest loan from a relative, but whatever the case, a capital infusion from someone close can often mean the difference between launching and flailing. Ready money and sweet deals are hard to find, especially when startups have no track record, little or no sales, little equity, and often no collateral. They have an enthusiastic entrepreneur with a super idea, many promises, and even more hope. But since hope doesn't pay the bills and charisma cannot collateralize a loan, mom, and dad are often the funding choice of first and last resort. Thus, it is not hard to understand why people turn to family and friends. However, from my experience, money from people who love you can be more of a mirage than a watering hole if it isn't handled correctly. That is because if you treat a business investment from someone close to you with all the seriousness it deserves and repay it promptly, it is indeed a gift from the gods. But if you are too casual about the arrangement (and many entrepreneurs who receive family funding are), you can cause stress to yourself and, worse yet, the people who believe in you. If something is too good to be true, it is. But if you are intelligent, prudent, and professional, all can go well.

- **Angel investors:** Google is an excellent example of a company that uses angel investing. The domain was not registered until 1997, and the company did not incorporate it until 1998. The reason was that Page and Brin met Andy Bechtolsheim in 1998, gave him a demonstration of Google, and decided to invest $100,000 in their developing company. Today, the rest is history. That $100,000 angel investment by Bechtolsheim soon led to almost another million in investor funding. In 1999, the venture capital firms Kleiner Perkins Caufield & Byers and Sequoia Capital helped raise $25 million for Google. In 2004, Google went public and raised more than $1 billion. Today, Google has been calculated to be the world's most valuable brand, with around $100 billion in revenue. Of course, this is a unique story because there is only one Google. Still, it is also a familiar story: A savvy investor can see an opportunity in your business idea, bet on it, and be convinced it will pay off handsomely—that's angel investing.

- **Venture capital:** Venture capital (VC) is the big time for getting the funding you need for your business. It is on Broadway. It is Showtime. Getting VC funding is difficult but can improve your business and career. An entrepreneur is said to be willing to take a risk with money to make money. If so, it might also be noted that a venture capitalist is an uber-entrepreneur and a super-capitalist since a venture capitalist is a person who bets big on new business ventures with colossal upside and equal upside risk. They invest millions in other people's money and are, therefore, looking for a significant rate of return for the firm on any deal with tremendous upside potential.

- **Banks and credit unions:** Other sources people usually consider when seeking outside funding for their business are banks and credit unions, and that makes sense. These institutions are lending money; they are good at it, and commercial lending is a bank's bread and butter. Banks especially like business credits because business loans are typically larger than personal loans, and the risk is usually more negligible. Your ability to get a commercial loan from a bank depends on many factors, the most important being the type of business you need the money for.

- **Crowdfunding:** Until now, we have looked at various ways to get people to believe in you and invest in your business, and in every one of those ways, the person making the investment and commitment of money expects to be paid back with cash. But not this time; crowdfunding is different. In crowdfunding, some businesses or projects need a certain amount of capital to move forward. Crowdfunding investors accept other types of rewards as payment instead of cash. Rewards are usually business or project-related.

- **Grants** are a sum of money given to an individual or business for a specific project or purpose to assist in developing the business. Therefore, they will be linked to a particular area of activity, such as training, new product development, or investment in plant and equipment. While grants may not cover the total costs of the project or purpose, the advantages of this type of funding are that as long as you fulfill any conditions attached to it, you will not have to repay it as you would with a loan, nor will you have to give up any shares in your business, as you would with an equity investor.

Whatever sources you eventually use to fund your business, there will always be some things you can do to ensure you get fully funded. And make no mistake about it—not having all the money you need seriously damages your ability to successfully execute your plans.

What Investors Look for Before Funding Your Business

Often, entrepreneurs with startups or new businesses turn to the bank for an overdraft when they need extra funding, forgetting that this arrangement is suitable only for short-term use. You want to look at finance mediums with longer terms, as that is what you need to get started. But before you seek funding for your new business from investors, you must prepare yourself and the company to meet these terms—it doesn't matter what type of financial injection you seek for your business.

- **The owners:** Are the owners or team seen as credible, capable, competent, and honest? Do they communicate effectively? What makes their idea unique? Do they have a suitable employment and financial or business history track record? Do they have the skills, knowledge, experience, and the right attitudes to make the business successful? Some investors might also be concerned with how much of the owner's money will be put into the company compared to the fund. Depending on the economic climate and type of business, most investors prefer not to lend more than 50% of the total capital required. However, this percentage may increase due to certain guarantees.

- **Business plan:** Do you have a business plan with reasonable business forecasts presented professionally? What's your business value proposition? How about listing your marketing and sales method alongside your specific customer target market? If the telephone is not ringing and email and texts are not flowing with date requests, you must do something to facilitate a relationship. Investors would also want to know your profit goals and competitive advantage.

- **Know your numbers:** The greater the depth of your market research, the more reliable your figures are. A precise definition of market research is systematic problem-analysis, model-building, and fact-finding to make better decisions and control the marketing of goods and services. Doing proper market research will help you know your numbers to monitor the effectiveness of your strategies.

- **Ensure your business is ready:** Is your business prepared for investing? Well, that depends on where you are in the industry and the funding cycle. The usual funding process will require a strong passion for the idea, a willingness to take risks, a good business plan, and motivation to keep the entrepreneurial spirit alive. Things, mostly. Getting turned down by a bank, getting an SBA loan. After that, if smooth sailing and growth continue, and you want it, you can go on to look for capital.

- **A clear investment structure:** Building a robust and friendly alliance with your lenders is essential. As most credit firms and savvy investors have business advisers to assist you in setting up your bank account, it shouldn't be too hard to find one with whom to build a relationship. Working together can tackle challenges as they arise and resolve potential problems before they become actual problems. Any expected difficulties could affect how you meet your obligations, so tell your lender in advance, not when it's too late. Provided you keep your lender regularly informed, notifying them of good times and bad times, they will listen and gladly assist you through any difficult patches you encounter.

When seeking funds for your business, the amount you need to borrow depends on the shortfall you discovered when you produced your cash flow forecast. While deciding on how much money you will need to buy equipment or premises is relatively easy, determining the amount of money you'll need to cover gaps between your income and expenditure might be more complex. However, you don't have to rely on one financial source. Each funding source has facilities to meet different requirements, so perhaps a combination of funding sources will prove right for you.

Action Points

1. What business idea do you have in mind?

____

____

____

2. What type of capital do you need to get the business off the ground?

____

____

3. Do you have a business plan in place yet?

4. What funding sources do you think best match your business plan?

"The dream is free. The hustle is sold separately." – Tyrese Gibson

CHAPTER SEVENTEEN

Managing a Business alongside a 9-5

Aside from discovering your inner strength and knowing how to harness your power, you have also probably established that you want a better career that will bring true satisfaction. However, quitting your current 9-5 job can be awkward when starting a new business. You might wonder if you should leave immediately or stay with the company until your business succeeds. Each person's situation is different; your answers to the above questions depend on your immediate needs and obligations. You want to examine your situation before making any final decisions. Before you begin planning what will work best for you, let me share my experience with a friend who didn't want to quit his job but needed to make extra money. This will help you review your options and make better decisions.

Fred is an office worker in a big publishing company. Of course, he liked his job but wanted to enjoy a larger paycheck. That year, the prospects for a raise looked bleak for everyone, but Fred pondered what he would tell his son when he asked about summer camp and how he would tell his daughter that he had a tight budget for her ballet lessons. Fred also had credit and had made a New Year resolution to pay off his credit cards faster and end the year debt-free. He met with me several days later, complaining about his predicament and how I could help him scale through. And the best advice I could give him was that he needed an additional source of income. I recommended that he create a side hustle income to reward himself with a more secure financial future.

Any hardworking and dedicated person who works as a salaried or hourly wage employee for someone else but wants to enjoy the benefits of earning more money on the side could start a side hustle and, eventually, a full-time business. You could even be a stay-at-home mom with kids to care for, an energetic teenager looking for ways to earn a little spending money or start a savings account, a college student who needs a way to stretch their tuition loans or a retired personnel who isn't ready to stay away from the business world for good. Even people who make a top salary enjoy the freedom and excitement of having a side hustle business. Perhaps you don't have to struggle to pay your essential bills, but wouldn't it be nice to have extra money for a trip to Hawaii this year instead of a long weekend in your state?

After a long week of tutorship with me, Fred understood all it takes to manage a business alongside his 9-5 job. He would get up every Saturday morning and go into his spare bedroom, and for two or three hours every week, he ran his teeny-tiny, one-book publishing company. He was making between $100 and $300, depending on the number of orders he got. He would spend time opening orders, addressing and filling envelopes with copies of his self-published DIY projects book, answering mail from readers, sending out press packets to generate publicity, endorsing checks, and (the best part) filling out a bank deposit. He ran the side hustle business for a few years, after which he established an empire. He once told me how he couldn't imagine the day he was not actively pursuing a small business on the side, regardless of his salary income. "Few things are as satisfying as a dollar earned on your own, by your talent and effort," Fred said.

Whether you should work or not and set up a business are all part of the larger question you face when caring for yourself, your family, and your home. What is important is that your choices are, at least, acceptable to you and your family and, at best, that they are wholeheartedly supported by those close to you. Not everyone will agree with your decision or support your desire to set up a business. The trick is to listen enough to people you trust to make an informed and sensible decision but not to let them decide for you. Once you take the bold step to start your own business, you can leverage the strategies I have shared in the next section to establish a secondary income source while still holding on to your current job.

How to Grow a Business Alongside Your Regular Job

Your situation will determine your choices when managing a business alongside a 9-5 job. Please remember that this journey is not about starting your new business as fast as possible; it is about finding what will make you happy and getting yourself into a position to obtain and hold on to that happiness. Here's how to grow a business alongside a 9-to-5 job:

- **Have designated times:** Effective time users can decide between efficiency and inefficiency. The natural growth of an organization makes the most of your time and energy. Some are highly organized, but many are confused by the work and demands of others. They are usually confused and stressed and feel that no matter how much guidance they need, they cannot take the time to clean up their lives. But organizing how you use your time is not as complicated as it seems, and it will reduce a great deal of stress. It involves scheduling your time for all the activities you want to do. Having designated times can transform your daily, weekly, monthly, and yearly goals, objectives, and tasks into a coordinated whole.

- **Be disciplined**: If you cannot be held to your word, you cannot have much meaning. When you commit to something, you are expected to stay engaged. No commitment has any significance unless it is honored. A commitment is a pledge, an obligation, or a promise that has to be kept, but this restricts freedom, and discipline is all about limitations. To be disciplined is to be refined too. When you honor your commitments to your new business, you become disciplined. Although honoring commitments takes more dedication and determination, no meaningful success can result from indiscipline. If you cannot control yourself, you can also not manage your business.

- **Create batches:** In our complex business world, you can't wait to achieve one long-term goal before moving on to the next. You will be working on short-term objectives that relate to multiple long-term goals and objectives at any time. So, how do you decide what to do first? You create batches and prioritize your tasks. To determine which studies are more critical than others, you must clearly understand each lesson.

- **Automate processes:** For instance, you can mention which hour you return calls so they know when to expect your call. You can ask callers to leave a message and tell you the best time to call them back, reducing the chances of a phone tag. You can also mention whom to call for immediate assistance and whom to call for other issues; for example, if people often call you when they really should be calling your coworker, provide that person's contact information. Another instance is when you need to stop working on a project, post a sticky note on the file or paperwork so that when you resume work on it, you will know precisely what the next step is, and you won't have to spend any time backtracking.

- **Balance your 9 to 5:** "But I don't have time! If only there were 36 hours in the day." How many times have you said those words to yourself? This is something people who are achieving less than their expectations usually say. But you need to understand that everyone—no matter how rich or poor, intelligent or ignorant, accomplished or unskilled—has the same 24 hours a day, 365 days a year.

Businesses You Can Build at 5 p.m.

While there are several business books out there promising that you can successfully quit your job and support yourself and your family with a business of your own, it's too risky, especially in today's challenging economy and with the spring-loaded job market. It's better to hang on to your job and use your free time to generate that much-needed second income. And if the unthinkable happens and you or your partner loses a full-time job, you will be in a much better cash position until you find another. Like my friend Fred, you might one day find that you can develop the extra-income business into a full-time pursuit with more significant earnings potential than what you are paid to do for someone else. Weekends, evenings, and quiet early morning hours can be turned into a newfound cash machine as you seek out new money-making opportunities, some of which I have shared here.

– **Pet sitting**: With so many busy professionals taking off on business trips regularly, who has time to care for the dog? Pet sitting is an easy-to-start business that works well for a weekend entrepreneur. "Animal sitting is also great for people who do jobs with flexible hours. Many pet owners don't want their beloved doggy to stay alone at night while they are gone. Strange, but true."

- **Custom gardening:** Custom gardening is ideal for entrepreneurs with a flair for growing. However, it is hard and dirty work and ultimately rewarding for garden lovers. You can attract clients through flyers, adverts, and wide publicity. Organic gardening and produce are hot right now, and I think things will continue improving.

- **Become a real estate agent's helper**: Real estate agents can't be everywhere at once, no matter how hard they try. Holding open houses, showing property, meeting with lenders, and prospecting for new clients—it's a steady job. To do a more efficient job, it is common for real estate agents to hire freelance assistants to help them with some of the less technical parts of their work.

- **Become a freelance illustrator:** Book publishing companies, magazines, newspapers, and websites all need images at various points. People will get used to it once you have a specific style down, so remain consistent. And don't think you need to be a world-class illustrator to make money from your drawings. It would help if you got yourself seen.

- **Children's party planning:** If you're the happiest when planning a party for a family member or even a coworker, and you live in an area where parents spend lots of money on their kids, you should think about starting a business where you can pay your time planning parties for kids. Of course, today's kids are pretty demanding, and a stint at the bowling alley or a trip to Disneyland will probably not cut it. So it's essential to know what boys and girls of different ages enjoy to help plan a successful party and boost your reputation.

- **Cleaning service:** Some business experts believe that a home and office cleaning business will be the fastest-growing service industry of the next ten years and that there will be no setup insight. Suppose you're thinking about starting a cleaning service. In that case, you can expect that once you hang up a simple card on the bulletin board at the supermarket offering your services, your phone will start to ring off the hook, and you'll probably be fully booked with more work than you can handle in just a few weeks.

It would help if you understood that staying with your current 9-5 job does not mean giving up on your dream for a better career. Instead, staying with your current job can be a helpful tool. For one thing, your job provides financial means to deal with expenditures. Your office might not be a happy place right now, but it gives some stability as you transition to exploring the entrepreneurial world. But to reduce time at a job you hate while continuously receiving a paycheck, approach your supervisors and ask them to reduce your hours to part-time. You do not need to tell them why you want your hours reduced; use "personal reasons" as an excuse. Though not all employers are willing to negotiate, it is an option to consider.

Action Points

1. Would you like to keep your day job and start a side hustle?

____
____
____

2. Which side hustle would you consider from the ones highlighted in this chapter?

____
____
____

3. How must you grow your business effectively without letting your current job suffer?

____
____
____

Conclusion

Now is the time to take up the challenge to change your business and life forever. Instead of sitting around wishing for more money, hundreds of thousands of people are doing something about it. They're starting their businesses. These are not unusual people with unique talents and unlimited funds to risk on new ventures. They are ordinary people with ordinary skills. But they share some “special ingredients”—plenty of enthusiasm for a business idea and a strong desire to succeed. Though starting a business is not for everyone, it can be a positive life change that can bring you professional pride and personal happiness.

Taking steps to become your boss and start a business might initially feel awkward; thus, you must explore the concept before committing mentally or monetarily. While there is no one guaranteed success formula, considering all the factors we have already discussed in this book will reduce your risk of failure. Of course, the journey can be short and sweet or long and arduous. No matter your method, it is essential to maintain a winning strategy throughout the entire career-changing process.

Although it is nice to believe each of us has innovative thoughts, this is not always true. If you think of a new business or service to the public, chances are someone is already delivering it elsewhere. It does not mean your idea is not profitable; instead, it proves that two or more people can concurrently have the same good idea.

Developing an idea that has already been done is not always problematic. For instance, if you live in a town that does not have a comic book store, other people have likely noticed a lack of comics, and it would not be surprising for two people to simultaneously open different comic book stores. Would that be a significant problem? Not completely. Yes, if you were to open one of the stores, you would have competition. Nevertheless, you would have to adjust what you sell so your store differs slightly from the other comic stores.

New businesses open up constantly to fulfill public needs. Because you are looking into a company you might run until it booms, you must complete this initial legwork before investing time, effort, or money into this project. As you brainstorm ideas, think back to careers you have had and enjoyed. Can you turn any of those past careers into a future business? Also, regardless of whether you provide goods or services, you do not have a business if you do not have customers. Heavy research about customers and potential markets should be done before starting any business—you can refer to Chapter 11, where I shared explicit details on conducting market analysis and keeping in touch with your customers. While doing your research, remain organized at all times.

In business, it's easy to do just enough. You are a winner if you win more times than you lose. For some, that may be enough. Having a business that employs people, invests in the capital, and creates living wages for you and others is honorable. If you picked up this book, though, you're yearning for more; you want to multiply your life and business 10x in the fastest way humanly possible and live a regret-free life. Every day, you have a choice. You can make your business small, or you can make it big.

Running a business makes you responsible and accountable for all decisions, thus forcing you to be available all hours, day and night. Establishing strict guidelines on what hours you will and will not work becomes a personal choice, and giving up personal commitments to run the business can become relatively easy. When selecting a company that will work well for you, decide what hours you prefer and how much effort you can afford. It is all right if, in the beginning, you need to work part-time for another company to make regular money while starting the business. It would help if you accepted that your business will take longer to flourish.

Furthermore, it would help if you put in twice the effort to do your part-time job and have energy for your privately owned business. Plus, you can expect extra time for personal obligations to reduce significantly during your first five years of business. Plan accordingly to keep your life in balance while running your business. If you commit to running a business, then save 110%. Running a business is not some hobby you put effort into on random occasions. It runs a substantial daily business with goals, deadlines, profit margins, and problems like every other business. You must be a motivated self-starter. Likewise, you have to be willing to continually seek training to better yourself and any present employees.

References

Alice, Voung. "Here's What Happens When You Don't Believe In Yourself." Live Your Life On Purpose, Medium, Oct. 25, 2019, https://medium.com/live-your-life-on-purpose/heres-what-happens-when-you-don-t-believe-in-yourself-a4970ae7f3cb.

Allison, Sue. "The 8 Areas of Life to Set Goals." CompassMyLife, https://www.compassmylife.com/areas-of-life-to-set-goals.

Brigitte, Hodge. "How to Organize Inventory for Small Businesses in 8 Steps." Reviewed by Meaghan Brophy, Fit Small Business, Sept. 8, 2021, https://fitsmallbusiness.com/inventory-management-for-small-business.

Charles, Duhigg. The Power of Habit: Why We Do What We Do in Life and Business. Random House Trade Paperbacks, 2012.

Dale, Carnegie. How To Win Friends And Influence People. Simon & Schuster, 1937.

Daniel, Goleman. Working with Emotional Intelligence. Bloomsbury, 1998.

Jinny, Ditzler. Your Best Year Yet. Thorsons, 1994.

Viktor, Frankl. Man's Search for Meaning. Verlag für Jugend und Volk, 1947.

Mark, Pentecost. "4 Ways Saying 'No' Can Improve Your Business." The Business Journals, Jul 5, 2016. https://www.bizjournals.com/bizjournals/how-to/growth-strategies/2016/07.

Mihaly, Csikszemmihalyi. Plow - The Psychology of Optimal Experience. Harper Perennial, 1991.

Paul, Coelho. Veronika Decides to Die. HarperCollins, 1998.

Robert, Kiyosaki. Rich Dad, Poor Dad. Warner, 1997.

Sarah, Ban. Simple Abundance. Bantam, 1995.

Stephen, Covey. First Things First. Simon & Schuster, 1994.

Stephen, Covey. The 7 Habits of Highly Effective People. Simon & Schuster, 1989.

Marie, Kondo. The Life-Changing Magic of Tidying Up. CreateSpace Independent Publishing Platform, 2017.

Young Entrepreneur Council. "Seven Ways To Cultivate Innovation And Creativity In Business." YEC Women Council Post, Forbes, March 13, 2018, https://www.forbes.com/sites/yec/2018/03/13/seven-ways-to-cultivate-innovation-and-creativity-in-business/?sh=5e4257d62336.

Made in the USA
Monee, IL
11 November 2026

1cdedb86-31d9-45f2-9e92-95780b1ac7d1R01